Greenup County, Kentucky

NATURALIZATIONS

REVOLUTIONARY WAR PENSIONS

LUNACY INQUESTS

1804–1902

Patricia Porter Phillips

HERITAGE BOOKS
2019

HERITAGE BOOKS
AN IMPRINT OF HERITAGE BOOKS, INC.

Books, CDs, and more—Worldwide

For our listing of thousands of titles see our website
at
www.HeritageBooks.com

Published 2019 by
HERITAGE BOOKS, INC.
Publishing Division
5810 Ruatan Street
Berwyn Heights, Md. 20740

Heritage Books by the author:

Greenup County, Kentucky Marriages: The First 100 Years, 1803–1903, A–K

Greenup County, Kentucky Marriages: The First 100 Years, 1803–1903, L–Z

Greenup County, Kentucky Naturalizations, Revolutionary War Pensions, Lunacy Inquests, 1804–1902

Greenup County, Kentucky Will Abstracts, 1822–1860

International Standard Book Numbers
Paperbound: 978-0-7884-0243-2
Clothbound: 978-0-7884-6155-2

TABLE OF CONTENTS

GREENUP COUNTY COURT ORDER BOOKS
(Office of County Court Clerk)

The County Order Books located in the Greenup County Court Clerk's Office are labeled as to the years covered; however, for convenience I have designated each book as a number (1-19) and use these numbers to indicate the Order Book for each quote given in the following text, i.e., Book 3, page 49 is given as 3/49, and is followed by the date of entry in the Court record. Several of the County Court Order Books were lost over the years, and I have noted these as "missing" in the following listing:

(1) 1804-1813 (missing)

(2) 1813-1818
     (Jan. 18, 1813 to June 22, 1818)

(3) 1818-1822 (missing)

(4) 1822-1827
     (June 10, 1822 to March 5, 1827)

(5) 1827-???? (missing)

(6) ????-1838 (missing)

(7) 1838-1846
     (August 3, 1838 to Sept. 7, 1846)

(8) 1846-1851
     (Oct. 5, 1846 to Nov. 3, 1851)

(9) 1851-???? (missing)

(10) ????-1857 (missing)

(11) 1857-1860
     (Jan. 5, 1857 to Feb. 6, 1860)

(12) 1860-1863
     (March 5, 1860 to Sept. 26, 1863)

(13) 1863-???? (missing)

(14)   ????-1869 (missing)

(15)   1869-1873
        (May 3, 1869 to July 14, 1873)

(16)   1873-1878
        (Aug. 4, 1873 to Aug. 26, 1878)

(17)   1878-1886
        (Sept. 2, 1878 to August 3, 1886)

(18)   1886-1894
        (Sept. 4, 1886 to June 25, 1894)

(19)   1894-???? (missing)

GREENUP CIRCUIT COURT ORDER BOOKS
(Office of Circuit Court Clerk)

Book A: April 16, 1804 to March 22, 1809

Book B: July 17, 1809 to July 23, 1814

Book C: October 17, 1814 to April 4, 1817

Book D: April 5, 1817 to July 6, 1818

Book E: April 27, 1820 to August 17, 1825
          Lawsuits on Land Grants and proving
          patents

Book Eo: October 6, 1818 - August 3, 1820

Book F: October 23, 1820 to October 4, 1824

Book G: October 1, 1824 to July 5, 1828

Book H: October 1, 1828 to April 5, 1832

Book I: July 1, 1832 to July 5, 1835

Book J: July 1835 to Sept. 1835 (missing)

Book K: September 24, 1835 to July 9, 1837

Book L: October 1, 1837 to July 2, 1839

Book M: October 1, 1839 to July 6, 1841

Book N: October 1, 1841 to April 4, 1844

Book O: April 5, 1844 to Oct. 6, 1847

Book P: April 24, 1848 to April 5, 1851

Book Q: June 6, 1851 to May 12, 1854

Book R: Nov. 1, 1854 to Dec. 1, 1855

Book S: May 12, 1856 to July 5, 1857

Book T: Nov. 9, 1857 to Nov. 24, 1858

Book U: November 24, 1858 to May 24, 1860

Book V: May 13, 1860 to May 27, 1862

Book W: July 21, 1862 to July 23, 1863

Book X: Nov. 9, 1863 to Sept. 13, 1865

Book Y: March 5, 1866 to Sept. 13, 1867

Book Z: Dec. 12, 1867 to Sept. 18, 1869

Book 26:   March 7, 1870 to March 21, 1871

Book 27:   Sept. 4, 1871 to Sept. 18, 1872

Book 28:   March 3, 1873 to Sept. 8, 1873

Book 29:   Sept. 8, 1873 to Sept. 10, 1873

Book 30:   Sept. 11, 1874 to March 17, 1875

Book 31:   March 18, 1875 to Sept. 15, 1876

Book 32:   March 5, 1877 to March 6, 1879

Book 33:   August 25, 1879 to Sept. 6, 1881

Book 34:   Feb. 27, 1882 to Sept. 11, 1884

Book 35:   Feb. 23, 1885 to Feb. 12, 1888

Book 36:   August 27, 1888 to Feb. 25, 1892

Book 37:   August 22, 1892 to April 17, 1896

Book 38:   July 20, 1896 to April 14, 1899

Book 39:   July 17, 1899 to October 6, 1902

NATURALIZATIONS

Anderson, George: Town of Dansick on the Baltick Pursan (sic) in Europe. U/203: 1st papers - July 19, 1859. Came to U.S. February 1826 from the town of Dansick on the Baltick Pursan in Europe.

Apps, James: Great Britain. Eo/529: 1st papers - August 3, 1820. Aged 29 years, about five feet seven and a quarter high, sandy hair, blue eyes, late a subject of Great Britain from the County of Kent, Dartford Parish in the Island of Great Britain. G/281: final papers - October 3, 1826.

Atkinson, Jonathan: England. N/240: 1st and final papers - October 4, 1842. Born in Kingdom of Great Britain; about 23 years of age; has been 11 years in United States of America; about 5' 2" high, hazel eyes, light hair, and of bright complexion.

Bambeck (Baback), Adam: Germany. P/9: 1st papers - April 24, 1848. By birth a German, 5'6" high, blue eyes, black hair--thinning grey, about 41 years old. P/319: final papers - October 28, 1850.

Baisch, Galleib Wm.: Wurtemburg, Germany. 1st papers - April 14, 1852 - Hamilton County, Ohio. T/415: final papers - July 19, 1858.

Barnet, Daniel: Great Britain. P/460: final papers - April 30, 1851.

Barnes, William: England. F/160: 1st papers - April 27, 1821. Born in the Parish of Charbray in the County of Curry in the Kingdom of Great Britain in that part of it called England; emigrated from that country in March 1818 and arrived at Philadephia in the United States on or about 29th day of May 1818; now resides in the town of Greenupsburg in the County of Greenup; aged 32 years; about 5' 9" high, black hair, dark complexion and black eyes.

Bartels, Wilhelm: Ireland and Britain. 1st papers - October 14, 1851 - place not given. S/473: final papers - July 20, 1857.

Bayless (Bayles), James: Great Britain and Ireland. 1st papers - October 31, 1855 - Greenup Circuit (not found). 12/41: final papers - April 27, 1860.

Berber, Robert: Great Britain. Eo/220: 1st papers - July 28, 1819. Aged 30 years, about 5'8" high, dark hair, black eyes and straight limbs; from the County of Northumberland in the Island of Great Britain.

Bernard, Charles Benedict: France. F/501: 1st papers - July 5, 1824. Born 14 October 1794 County of Neufchattel in Switzerland; when he was about 5 his father removed with him to town of Pontarlier in France; at the age of 14 years he was taken into the service of Napoleon, Emperor, where he remained four years and upwards; that in the year 1812 he left the service of the Emperor Napoleon and came to United States where he arrived in 1813, having been upwards of a year on sea, and that he has resided ever since in the United States and the last three years in the state of Kentucky.

Boyle, John: Great Britain & Ireland. R/207: final papers - May 21, 1855.

Brabeck, Sebastian: Bavaria, Germany. 1st papers - February 22, 1856 - Court of Common Pleas, Marion County, Missouri. 12/42: final papers - May 2, 1860.

Bradey, Henry: Great Britain and Ireland. 1st papers - February 7, 1856 - Common Pleas in the State of Ohio. T/415: final papers - July 19, 1858.

Branagem, John: Mahad, Ireland. U/49: 1st papers - May 13, 1859. Arrived U.S. August 7, 1856 from the County of Mahad in Ireland.

Breming, Frank: Prussia. 1st papers - September 23, 1857 - Court of Common Pleas of Ohio. U/257: final papers - November 14, 1859.

Brogan, Thomas: Ireland. 1st papers - September 4, 1855 - place not given. 16/267: final papers - August 3, 1876.

Bromo, William: England. Eo/221: 1st papers - July 28, 1819. Aged 21 years, about 5'10" high, dark hair, blue eyes, straight limbs; from County of Northumberland, Rolh Cury Parrish in the Island of Great Britain.

Brown, Andrew: Scotland. Eo/528: 1st papers - August 3, 1820. 28 years, 5'8" high, light hair and blue eyes; County of Fyffe, Parish of Crail in that part of Great Britain called Scotland in the Island of Great Britain.

Burgraf, John: Bavaria, Germany. P/194: 1st papers - April 27, 1849. Came to U.S. 12 years ago; 5'8" high, heavy made, fair hair, grey eyes, light complexion.

Burgraf, Lucas: Bavaria, Germany. 1st papers - February 24, 1857 - Court of Common Pleas, Hamilton County, Ohio. 12/27: final papers - April 2, 1860.

Burhardt, Lewis: Switzerland. 15/131: 1st and final papers - August 1, 1870. Came to United States as a minor under the age of 21.

Burk, John: Great Britain and Ireland. R/208: 1st papers - June 21, 1856. U/49: final papers - May 13, 1859.

Burke, Michael: Ireland. S/176: final papers - November 10, 1856.

Burkhardt, Rudolph: Switzerland. 15/119: 1st papers - June 6, 1870. Imigrated to United States in 1854 and landed at New York in the State of New York in the year 1854; is 50 years of age, and has resided in Greenup County, Kentucky about 13 years last past.

Burkheart, Sigmund: Switzerland. 15/266: 1st and final papers - August 7, 1871. Came to United States under age 21, resided one year in Kentucky.

Busel (Bussell) John: Bavaria, Germany. P/158: 1st papers - April 23, 1849. Came to U.S. in September or October 1845. P/482: final papers - May 2, 1851.

Bushfield, James: Ireland. I/287: 1st papers - July 18, 1834. A native of Ireland, who is about 30 years of age, has been a resident and citizen of Greenup for about 9 years; 6 ft. high, fair complexion, blue eyes, fair hair.

Bustetter, Harmon: Grand Duchy of Baden, Germany. 15/130: 1st papers - July 18, 1870. Came to United States December 1, 1865 from Baden. 15/353: final papers - August 5, 1872.

Burtenshaw, Thomas: England. O/28: 1st papers - October 8, 1844. P/110: final papers - October 26, 1848. P/430: final papers - April 28, 1851. NOTE: P/110 and P/430 appear to be the same person; P/110 refers to first papers in October 1845 term. (No papers were filed in October 1845 term of Circuit Court; however, papers were filed in the October 1844 term.) P/430 states only that he "had previously stated his intention."

Caden, Lewis: Germany. R/103: 1st papers - November 23, 1854. Emigrated to U.S. 1850 from Germany and landed in New York, at which time he was under 18 years of age, and has since resided in Kentucky and Virginia and for the last 2 years in County of Greenup.

Callings, William K.: Great Britain. P/8: 1st papers - April 24, 1848. By birth a subject of Queen Victoria, Soverign of Great Britain; about 51 years old and about 6 feet high.

Clark, Robert: England. 1st papers - October 9, 1844 - Court of Common Pleas of the State of Ohio. O/395: final papers - October 25,

1847. 5' 9 1/2" in height, black hair, hazel
eyes, and about 26 years of age.

Clary, Timothy: Ireland. P/108: 1st papers -
October 26, 1848. Came to U.S. August 1838
from Ireland. S/269: final papers - November
22, 1856.

Coleman, John J.: Germany. T/192: 1st
papers - May 10, 1858. Came to U.S. when an
infant; is now 22 years of age and resided
in United States since his earliest recollec-
tion; born in Germany, but in which of the
German States he does not know.

Connell, Patrick: Britain. 1st papers - August
15, 1857 - Court of Common Pleas, Lawrence
County, Ohio. U/386: final papers - November
26, 1859.

Cripple, Bernhardt: Germany. 15/50: 1st
papers - November 1, 1869. Came to United
States about 1849 from Germany.

Currick, James: Great Britain and Ireland.
1st papers - August 15, 1857 - Court of Common
Pleas Lawrence County, Ohio. U/386: final
papers - November 26, 1859.

Daugherty, John: Britain and Ireland. S/156:
final papers - July 22, 1856.

Deatz, John: Wurtemburg, Germany. P/90: 1st
papers - October 24, 1848. About 29 years
old, 5'8" high, blue eyes and sharp nose; came
to United States from Wurtemburg.

Deickman, Casper H.: Prussia. 1st papers -
September 3, 1886 - place not given. 18/150:
final papers - October 1, 1888.

Deterick, William: Hanover, Germany. 1st
papers - July 19, 1858 - Greenup Circuit (not
found). 12/89: final papers - August 3, 1860.

Diederichs, Fredick: Hanover, Germany. 1st
papers - May 22, 1854 - Circuit Court of Maryland. T/415: final papers - July 19, 1858.

Dillen, Patrick: Great Britain. 1st papers - October 13, 1866 - Marshall Circuit Court, Indiana. 15/12: final papers - June 2, 1869.

Doogan, Hugh: Great Britain and Ireland. 1st papers - September 26, 1856 - Court of Common Pleas, Lawrence County, Ohio. 12/30: final papers - April 2, 1860.

Doyle, Patrick: Britain and Ireland. 1st papers April 26, 1856 - Circuit Court of Carter County, Kentucky. T/370: final papers - May 25, 1858.

Dugan, Daniel: Great Britain and Ireland. 1st papers - March 25, 1858 - Court of Common Pleas, Lawrence County, Ohio. 12/33: final papers - April 2, 1860.

Dugan, Matthew: Ireland. 15/271: 1st and final papers - September 4, 1871. Came to United States on August 16, 1849 from the County of Galway, Ireland, under the age of 15 years.

Durnda (Durrda), George: Hanover, Germany. 1st papers - February 13, 1854 - place not given. U/286: final - November 18, 1859.

Dunda, Henry: Hanover, Germany. 1st papers - February 13, 1854 - Court of Common Pleas of Scioto County, Ohio. U/17: final papers - May 9, 1859.

Edwards, David: Great Britain. 1st papers - July 11, 1836 - Common Pleas County of Allegheny in the State of Pennsylvania. N/186: final papers - July 6, 1842.

Eich, Englebert: Prussia. 15/145: 1st papers - August 29, 1870. Came to United States on August 1, 1863 from the Kingdom of Prussia.

Eichler, Joseph: Baden, Germany. R/206: 1st papers - May 21, 1855. Came to U.S. July 28, 1853 from Grand Duchy of Baden in Germany.

Elms (Ellams), James: Britain. P/194: 1st papers - April 27, 1849. Came to U.S. 1839 from England; 5'4" high, dark skin, slight beard and 44 years of age. P/460: final papers - April 30, 1851.

Emmon, Joseph: Baden, Germany. 12/29: 1st papers - April 2, 1860. Came to United States on the 30th day of June 1852 from the County of Baden in Germany.

Enka, August: Hanover, Germany. 1st papers - September 6, 1858 - Greenup Circuit Court (not found). 12/89: final papers - August 3, 1860.

Evans, Griffith: South Wales. M/139: 1st papers - April 11, 1840. Born in the County of Glamorgshire, South Wales; about 34 years of age; has been 8 years in the United States of America; about 5' 10" high, hazel eyes, sandy hair and bright complexion.

Farson, Frank W.: Prussia. 1st papers - September 3, 1886 - place not given. 18/150: final papers - October 1, 1888.

Fearing, A. Kit (AKit): Baden, Germany. 18/40: 1st and final papers - April 23, 1860. Came to United States on or about January 11, 1852 from the Grand Duchy of Baden in Germany, that he was under the age of 18 years when he came to United States.

Fenirty, Richard: Ireland. 15/122: 1st papers - July 5, 1870. Came to United States on 22nd day of April 1862 from the County King in Ireland. 28/62: March 10, 1873 - final papers.

Ferry, Michael: Ireland. S/176: final papers - November 10, 1856.

Fetter, Peter: Hese Darmstadt, Germany. M/248: 1st and final papers (signed July 9, 1840) filed with Court July 10, 1840. About 25 years of age, 5' 4 1/2" high, light hair, hazel eyes and of bright complexion; been 8 years in the United States of America and 3 years in State of Kentucky.

Fetter, Nicholas: Germany. M/139: 1st and
final papers - April 11, 1840. Born in Germany;
about 23 years of age; has been 8 years in
United States of America; about 5' 4" high,
hazel eyes, light hair, and of bright complexion.

Fielink, Lewis: Holland. 1st papers - September
30, 1844 - Court of Common Pleas of the State
of Ohio. O/410: final papers - October 25,
1847.   5'7" high, 160 lbs., inclines slighty
to be sandy complexion, 36 years of age, two
teeth out above on the right side, fair skin.

Fillmeyer, Christopher: Britain & Ireland.
1st papers: July 21, 1855 - place not given.
S/473: final papers - July 20, 1857.

Fisher, George: Bavaria, Germany. P/90: 1st
papers - October 24, 1848. Age 17 years, dark
skin, blue eyes, light hair and a round face;
came to United States from Kingdom of Bavaria.

Flack, Andrew: Prussia. 1st papers - April
13, 1880 - place not given. 17/131: final
papers - June 5, 1882.

Flinn, Andrew: Ireland. H/457: 1st papers -
April 4, 1832. Born in the County of Lietrim,
Ireland; about 40 years of age; has been 22
years in the United States of America; 5' 5
1/2" high, hazel eyes, brown hair mixed with
grey and of dark complexion. I/203: final
papers - April 10, 1834.

Flinn, Martin: Ireland and Great Britain.
Q/279: 1st papers - November 18, 1852.

Francis, William: Ireland. H/150: 1st papers
- October 5, 1829. Aged about 35 years, about
5' 8" high, of a dark complexion and blue eyes,
who was born in Ireland.

Freel, Michael: Great Britain and Ireland.
1st papers - January 11, 1870 - Boyd County
Court, Boyd County, Kentucky. 15/349: final
papers - July 19, 1872.

Freil, James: Britain. 1st papers - September 22, 1853 - Court of Common Pleas State, of Pennsylvania. U/145: final papers - May 23, 1859.

Gallagher, Daniel: Great Britain & Ireland. R/207: final papers - May 21, 1855.

Gallaugher, William: Great Britain and Ireland. 1st papers - August 5, 1857 - Court of Common Pleas, Lawrence County, Ohio. 12/94: final papers - August 4, 1860.

Galt, Samuel: Great Britain. S/13: 1st and final papers - May 13, 1856. Came to United States at age 14.

Garthee, George: Great Britain. G/179: final papers - April 3, 1826. Resided County of Greenup upwards of three years last past.

Gavan (Gavin), Martin: Great Britian and Ireland. 1st papers - May 27, 1857 - Court of Common Pleas, Lawrence County, Ohio. 12/35: final papers - April 2, 1860.

Geiger, Henry: Hanover, Germany. 1st papers - May 22, 1854 - Circuit Court for the District of Maryland. T/414: final papers - July 19, 1858.

Gentil, Leonard: 1st papers - November 8, 1852 - Lawrence County, Ohio. 12/95: final papers - August 7, 1860.

Gerthe, George: Prussia. F/273: 1st papers - October 15, 1822. Born in Germany; about 30 years of age and 6 years in America; 5' 1" high, blue eyes, light hair and of fair complexion.

Gill, Edward: Ireland and Great Britain. 1st papers - July 4, 1851 - United States District Court in and for the District of Delaware. Q/150: final papers - May 19, 1852.

Gohsling, Frederick: Prussia. 1st papers - June 4, 1852 - Court of Common Pleas, Hamilton

County, Ohio. 12/35: final papers - April
2, 1860.

Golen, Peter: France. G/514: 1st papers -
July 11, 1828. Born in Versailles in France;
about 42 years of age; and has been in America
about 13 years; 5' 6" high, dark eyes, dark
hair, and of dark complexion.

Golliher, Edward: Great Britain & Ireland.
1st papers - May 21, 1855 - Greenup Circuit
Court (not found). T/352: final papers -
May 24, 1858.

Golliher, John: Great Britain & Ireland. 1st
papers - May 21, 1855 - Greenup Circuit Court
(not found). T/352: final papers - May 24,
1858.

Graber, Jacob: Wurtemburg, Germany. T/257:
1st papers - May 15, 1858 (signed May 14, 1858).
Came to United States November 2, 1851 from
the Kingdom of Wurtemburg, and is now 29 years
of age. V/11: final papers - May 29, 1860.

Grahn, K. B.: Hanover, Germany. 15/334: 1st
papers - May 6, 1872. Came to United States
on June 29, 1865 from the City of Hanover in
the Empire of Germany.

Griesbeck, George: Bavaria. 1st papers - August
29, 1853 - Circuit Court for the United States
for the Western District of Pennsylvania.
12/36: final papers - April 2, 1860.

Griffin, Michael: Ireland. R/492: 1st papers
- November 28, 1855. Came to United States
of America more than 4 years ago. 12/38: final
papers - April 2, 1860.

Gross, Sharran: Nassau. 1st papers - September
1, 1856 - Court of Common Pleas, Armstrong
County, Pennsylvania. 12/42: final papers -
May 2, 1860.

Grote, Conrad: Germany. P/142: 1st papers -
October 27, 1848. About 25 years of age, 5'6"
high, brown hair, light complexion and grey

eyes and well proportioned. Q/243: final papers - July 23, 1852.

Guilkey, Joseph: Prussia. 12/29: 1st and final papers - April 2, 1860. Came to United States while a minor, without father or mother, under 18 years of age and has resided ever since in the United States, being for the period of about 13 years.

Gwynn, Albert: England. 15/122: 1st papers - July 5, 1870. Came to United States March 28, 1865 from the County of Gloucestershire. 15/354: final papers - August 5, 1872.

Halley, Patrick: Great Britain & Ireland. Q/480: 1st papers - November 24, 1853. S/67: final papers - May 24, 1856.

Halley, Thomas: Great Britain & Ireland. R/438: final papers - November 21, 1855.

Hand, William: Saxon. S/483: 1st papers - July 21, 1857. 12/93: final papers - August 4, 1860.

Handlin, John: Great Britain. 1st papers - July 28, 1876 - Greenup County Court (not found). 16/420: final papers - July 29, 1878.

Hanaghan, John: Ireland. 15/368: 1st papers - October 7, 1872. Came to United States October 11, 1860 from the County of Mayo in Ireland. 16/267: final papers - August 3, 1876.

Hartman, Frank: Bavaria/Prussia. 1st papers - December 24, 1856 - Court of Common Pleas, Hamilton County, Ohio. 12/36: final papers - April 2, 1860.

Heelin, Patrick: Ireland. 15/27: 1st papers July 19, 1869. Came to United States August 12, 1863 from the County of Dawn in Ireland.

Heine, Henry: Prussia. 1st papers - May 9, 1870 - Court of Common Pleas, County of New York, State of New York. 16/162: final papers - June 7, 1875.

Heineman (Hineman), George: Baden, Germany.
15/129: 1st papers - July 18, 1870. Came
to United States July 1, 1867 from Baden.
15/352: final papers - August 3, 1872.

Henkes, Balthsar: Nassau. X/370: 1st and
final - July 20, 1865. Came to United States
when he was an infant about 14 years old and
has resided here ever since. He is now in
his 26th year.

Herress, Peter: Prussia. 1st papers -
November 9, 1870 - Greenup County Court (not
found). 15/453: final papers - June 2, 1873.

Hertel (Hartel), Jacob: Hess Darmstadt, City
of Erlael, Germany. L/120: 1st papers - April
6, 1838. 5' 8" high, about 40 years of age,
and with dark hair and black eyes. M/216:
final papers - July 8, 1840.

Highman, Henry: Hanover, Germany. W/18: 1st
papers - July 22, 1862 (signed July 21, 1862).
Came to United States 8 years ago; is about
48 years of age, 5' 7½" high, light complexion
and weighs about 130 pounds. X/193: final
papers - September 5, 1864.

Hilleben, George: Hanover, Germany. 1st papers
- March 24, 1857 - Court of Common Pleas, Scioto
County, Ohio. 12/90: final papers - August
3, 1860.

Hiterman (Heiterman), Joseph: Baden Township,
Germany. R/85: 1st papers - November 21,
1854 (signed November 20, 1854). In 1847 he
left Baden Township, Germany and landed in
New York August 1, 1847, lived in Pennsylvania
from 1847 to 1852; 1852 to latter part of 1853
lived at Stootenville, Ohio; has been one year
in Kentucky, mostly at Clinton Furnace. Now
lives at Pennsylvania Furnace in Greenup County.

Hooge, Andrew: Great Britain and Ireland.
12/99: 1st papers - August 7, 1860. Came
to United States on 1st day of May 1853 from
Canida (sic), one of the providences of Great
Britain.

Hosman, Frederick: Hanover, Germany. 1st papers - February 25, 1854. U/198: final papers - July 18, 1859.

Howell, John: Great Britain. P/470: final papers - May 1, 1851.

Hunker, Christian: Wurtimburg, Germany. 1st papers - June 5, 1855 - Court of Quarter Sessions of Allegheny County in the Commonwealth of Pennsylvania. 12/34: final papers - April 2, 1860.

Jones, Samuel: Flintshire, South Wales. L/238: 1st papers - October 2, 1838. Native of Flint-shire in the Kingdom of Wales, a part of Great Britain; age 31 years, 5' 6 1/2" high, thick set, hair neither light nor dark, light blue eyes, moderately fair skin and no other peculiar feature, dialect considerably Welsh. M/288: final papers - October 8, 1840.

Karl, Joseph: Bavaria, Germany. 12/44: 1st and final papers - May 2, 1860. Came to United States 1852 a minor under 18 years of age at the time of his arrival; resided State of Kentucky 6 years and for the last 2 years in the County of Greenup.

Karlty (Keatly), William: Great Britain. P/403: 1st papers - November 2, 1850. 30 years of age, 5'6" high, sandy complexion, sandy hair, blue eyes, 130 lbs.

Kassan, Augustus: Hanover, Germany. 1st papers - September 3, 1853 - place not given. T/408: final papers - July 19, 1858.

Kaut, John: Bavaria, Germany. 0/450: 1st papers - October 29, 1847. Came to United States June 15, 1839; 34 years old, about 5'11" high, brownish hair, hazel eyes dark skin and stoop shouldered. P/256: final papers - April 23, 1850.

Kelly, Henry: Ireland. March 16, 1818 - 1st papers - Gallia County Ohio, Court of Common Pleas. Born in Kilherney in the Kingdom of

Ireland, under the allegiance of the King of
Great Britain and emigrated from Ireland October
2, 1811; arrived at Niagara in the United States
of America on the 13th day of September 1813;
now resides in Rackoon in the County of Gallia
in the state of Ohio. F/84: final papers -
April 25, 1821.

Kelley, Martin: Britain. 1st papers - August
5, 1857 - Court of Common Pleas, Lawrence
County, Ohio. U/385: final papers - November
26, 1859.

Keller, Conrad: Baden, Germany. 1st papers -
March 21, 1857 - Court of Common Pleas, Scioto
County, Ohio. 12/31: final papers - April
2, 1860.

Kiner, John: Bavaria, Germany. 1st papers -
May 24, 1858 - Greenup Circuit Court (not
found). U/588: final papers - May 25, 1860.

Kinney, Michael: Great Britain & Ireland.
T/264: final papers - May 15, 1858.

Kinsler, Christian: Baden, Germany. R/415:
1st papers - July 25, 1855. Came to U.S. June
2, 1846 from the Grand Duchy of Baden in
Germany. T/287: final papers - May 18, 1858.

Kittern, Charles: Baden, Germany. 1st papers
- May 20, 1856 - Greenup Circuit Court (not
found). T/353: final papers - May 24, 1858.

Klaiber, John A.: Wurtemburg, Germany. 1st
papers - July 7, 1856 - Greenup Circuit Court
(not found). U/241: final papers - July 22,
1859.

Klauder, John: Hessen. S/287: final papers -
November 26, 1856.

Kline, George: Hanover, Germany. 1st papers -
September 3, 1855 - Greenup Circuit Court (not
found). T/417: final papers - July 20, 1858.

Kramer, Leonhard: Prussia. 1st papers - June
20, 1855 - Greenup Circuit Court (not found).
12/38: final papers - April 2, 1860.

Krone, Henry: Hanover, Germany. 1st papers -
September 13, 1858 - Greeenup Circuit (not
found). 12/127: final papers - November 5,
1860.

Krull, John H.: Hanover, Germany. 15/469:
1st and final papers - August 4, 1873. Came
to United States under age 21.

Kyle, Owen: England. 1st papers - March 18,
1850 - Court of Common Pleas, Blair County,
Pennsylvania. U/140: final papers - May 23,
1859.

Lasiman, William: Hanover, Germany. 1st
papers - May 19, 1856 - Greenup Circuit (not
found). 12/91: final papers - August 3, 1860.

Laverty, Adam: Ireland. 15/138: 1st papers -
August 19, 1870. Came to United States March
12, 1865 from the County of Antrim in Ireland.

Lawthers, Thomas: Ireland. Q/195: 1st papers
- May 22, 1852. Came to U.S. 1849.

Lessien, Michael: Britain. 1st papers -
November 7, 1857 - Court of Common Pleas,
Lawrence County, Ohio. U/385: final papers -
November 26, 1859.

Lewis, David: Wales. Q/216: 1st papers -
July 20, 1852. Is a citizen of Wales and has
been in United States 11 years past. R/358:
final papers - July 16, 1855.

Lewis, Edward: England. 15/419: 1st and
final papers - February 3, 1873. Came to United
States a minor under age 21.

Lewis, George W.: Great Britain and Ireland.
R/264: 1st papers - May 26, 1855. Came to
United States October 9, 1841, landed at New
York City.

Linsky, Martin: Great Britain and Ireland.
1st papers - August 5, 1857 - Common Pleas
Court of Lawrence County, Ohio. 11/321: final
papers - December 27, 1859.

Long, John: Germany. R/370: final papers - July 17, 1855.

Lonier, Gurge: Wurtemburg, Germany. 1st papers - May 29, 1857 - Court of Common Pleas, Lawrence County, Ohio. U/223: final papers - July 20, 1859.

Lundy, Peter: Ireland. Q/54: 1st papers - November 15, 1851. Came to United States 3 years last past.

Mack, Joseph: Baden, Germany. R/206: 1st papers - May 21, 1855. Came to United States October 5, 1848 from the Grand Duchy of Baden in Germany. S/391: final papers - May 21, 1857.

Malaney, Hugh: Ireland. 26/151: September 8, 1870 - 1st papers. Came to the United States on the ____ day of January 1866 from the County of Ruscomeron in Ireland.

Mapes, Charles: Saxon. R/422: final papers - November 19, 1855.

Marcus, Peter: Italy. 18/249: 1st papers - July 7, 1890. Came to United States in 1883 from Italy.

Martsee, Henry: Prussia. Q/589: final papers - May 23, 1854.

McBinn, Norman M.: Great Britain. Q/195: 1st papers - May 22, 1852. Came to U.S. in 1849 from Nova Scotia.

McCarran, William: Great Britain & Ireland. R/208: 1st papers - May 21, 1855. T/353: final papers - May 24, 1858.

McGarvey, Patrick: Ireland. S/422: 1st papers - May 23, 1857. Came to United States March 23, 1852 from Ireland. U/201: final papers - July 18, 1859.

McGuire, Owen: Ireland. 15/27: 1st papers - July 19, 1869. Came to United States May 9,

1864 from the County of Sligo in Ireland.
15/265: final papers - August 2, 1871.

McGunagle, James: Great Britain and Ireland.
1st papers - October 14, 1857 - Court of Common
Pleas, Lawrence County, Ohio. 12/34: final
papers - April 2, 1860.

McIntire, Darby: Great Britain & Ireland.
1st papers - 185___ - place not given. S/513:
final papers - July 24, 1857.

McKee, John: Great Britain & Ireland. Q/256:
1st papers - November 15, 1852. R/98: final
papers - November 22, 1854.

McKee, Thomas: Ireland. R/124: 1st and final
papers - November 25, 1854. Born in Ireland
on October 12, 1830; came to United States
on November 26, 1840.

Meinshausen, Heinrich: Hanover, Germany. 1st
papers - November 19, 1856 - Greenup Circuit
(not found). 12/322: final papers - August
4, 1862.

Meinshausen, Wilhelm: Hanover, Germany. 1st
papers - November 19, 1856 - Greenup Circuit
(not found). 12/322: final papers - August
4, 1862.

Meiser, John: Switzerland. 1st papers - April
16, 1853 - Court of Common Pleas, Alleghany
County, Pennsylvania. 15/123: final papers -
July 5, 1870.

Meredith, John - Brechnschshire, Wales. L/238:
1st papers - October 2, 1838. Age 45 years
on the 7th day of June last; 5' 7" high, moderately thick, hair dark and thick on his head,
hazel eyes, skin, beard and eyebrows dark,
dialect moderately plain English for a Welch
man.

Messer, John: Baden, Germany. 15/119: 1st
papers - June 6, 1870. Came to United States
about 19 years of age.

Millett, William: Ireland. S/386: 1st papers - November 20, 1857. Over 21 years of age, a native of Ireland, emigrated to United States of America and has been resident of United States for the last five years, continuously upon the 6th day of month; he landed at the Port of New York. U/197: final papers - July 18, 1859.

Mormin (Moraim), Daniel: Great Britain & Ireland. R/208: 1st papers - May 21, 1855. T/352: final papers - May 24, 1858.

Moreman, Joseph: Oldenburg. 1st papers - July 19, 1858 - Greenup Circuit Court (not found). W/29: final papers - July 23, 1862.

Moriarty, Patrick: Great Britain and Ireland. 1st papers - May 4, 1852 - Circuit Court of Mason County, Virginia. 12/31: final papers - April 2, 1860.

Mulherron, Daniel: Great Britain and Ireland. 1st papers - September 20, 1856 - Lawrence County, Ohio, Court of Common Pleas. 12/37: final papers - April 2, 1860.

Murphy, James: Great Britain and Ireland. 12/79: 1st and final papers - June 27, 1860. Came to United States in the Fall of 1852, and when he came here he was under the age of 18 years at the time of his arrival in the United States and has continued to reside therein ever since; has resided in the State of Kentucky for the last six years and that three years has resided in Carter, Greenup and Boyd Counties; now over 21 years of age.

Murray, Patrick: Great Britain and Ireland. R/208: 1st papers - May 21, 1855. T/351: final papers - May 24, 1858.

Myer, Charles: Baden, Germany. 12/45: 1st and final papers - May 2, 1860. Came to United States 1852, a minor under the age of 18 years at time of his arrival, resided the last 4 years in Greenup County.

Myers, Benjamin: Wurtemburg, Germany. U/286: 1st papers - November 18, 1859.

Nazer, Jacob: Weedenburg, Germany. 12/134: 1st and final papers - November 6, 1860. Came to United States a minor under age 21; has resided in the United States 5 years at least and in this state one year last past, during 3 years out of the 5 years he was a minor under the age of 21 years.

Nichols, Thomas: Great Britain. S/142: final papers - July 21, 1856.

Nickel, Joseph: Bayam. Q/55: 1st papers - November 19, 1851. Came to U.S. December 1844; 5'11" high, brown eyes and hair, blacksmith by trade, age 42. Q/442: final papers - November 21, 1853.

Nilty, Richard: Great Britain and Ireland. R/208: 1st papers - May 21, 1855.

Noonan, Daniel: Great Britain and Ireland. 1st papers - March 2, 1866 - Marquette County, Michigan. Z/4: final papers - March 2, 1868.

Norris, Charles: Ireland. F/273: 1st papers - October 15, 1822. Born in Dennegal, Ireland; about 23 years of age; 5'8" high, dark hair, light complexion and blue eyes; has been in United States better than 4 years. G/181: final papers - April 4, 1826.

O'Brian, George: Great Britain and Ireland. 1st papers - March 25, 1858 - Court of Common Pleas, Lawrence County, Ohio. 12/33: final papers - April 2, 1860.

O'Brien, Jerry: Ireland. 15/138: 1st papers - August 19, 1870. Came to United States August 5, 1865, from the County of Kirk in Ireland.

O'Brien, Michael: Great Britain and Ireland. 1st papers - November 19, 1856 - Greenup Circuit (not found). 12/113: final papers - October 7, 1860.

O'Connor, John: Ireland. R/131: 1st papers - November 27, 1854. Emigrated from Ireland to the City and State of New York on November 20, 1848.

O'Laughlin, Cornelius: Ireland. R/492: 1st papers - November 28, 1855. Came to United States more than 4 years ago.

Oltino, Angelo: Italy. 1st papers - August 6, 1888 - place not given. 18/275: final papers - November 3, 1890.

Oltino, John: Italy. 1st papers - August 6, 1888 - place not given. 18/274: final papers - November 3, 1890.

Oltino, Peter: Italy. 1st papers - August 6, 1888 - place not given. 18/274: final papers - November 3, 1890.

O'Neil (Oneal), Patrick: Ireland. R/209: 1st papers - May 21, 1855. S/415: final papers - May 23, 1857.

Osenton (Osten), Samuel: England. D/243: 1st papers - July 29, 1818. Aged 31 years; about 5' 7" high, light hair, blue eyes and straight limbs; late a subject of the King of Great Britain; from the City of London. Eo/529: final papers - August 3, 1820.

Otto, William: Hanover, Germany. W/18: 1st papers - July 22, 1862 (signed July 21, 1862). Native of Hanover, a German state, about 47 years old, 5' 3" high, fair complexion, and weighs about 124; has been in United States of America about 6 years. X/192: final papers - September 5, 1864.

Paih (Paik), Bernard: Prussia. O/410: 1st papers - October 25, 1847. Aged about 36 years, left Prussia October 1, 1844; arrived New Orleans about December 20, 1844.

Passenback, John: Bavaria, Germany. T/159: final papers - November 24, 1857.

Patterson, George: Great Britain. Eo/220: 1st papers - July 28, 1819. Aged 22 years; about 6'1" high, dark hair, blue eyes and straight limbs; from County of Northumberland, Parish of Rolh Cury, being in the Island of Great Britain.

Patterson, John: Great Britain. V/428: 1st papers - May 21, 1862. Been in the United States more than 5 years last past. X/238: final papers - September 9, 1864.

Patterson, Samuel: Ireland. P/194: 1st papers - April 27, 1849. 28 years old, 5'6" high, fair porportioned in size, hazel eyes, fair complexion, brown hair; came from Great Britain. P/430: final papers - April 28, 1851.

Patterson, Samuel: Ireland. R/357: 1st papers - July 16, 1855. Came to United States February 1846. T/409: final papers - July 19, 1858.

Patterson, William: Great Britain & England. O/28: 1st papers - October 8, 1844. O/352: final papers - April 27, 1847

Peff, Joseph: Baden, Germany. T/40: 1st papers - November 12, 1857. 12/112: final papers - October 7, 1860.

Phillips (Philips), Edmund: Ireland. M/36: 1st papers - October 10, 1839. Born in County of Maith, Ireland; about 26 years of age; has been 8 years in United States of America; about 5'7" high, hazel eyes, brown hair, and of fair complexion. M/37: final papers - October 10, 1839.

Pritt, Thomas: Great Britain and Ireland. Q/279: 1st papers - November 18, 1852.

Rainer, John: Germany. 1st papers - October 18, 1854, Court of Common Pleas, Vinton County, Ohio. 12/30: final papers - April 2, 1860.

Raisch, Godfried: Wurtemburg, Germany. S/73: final papers - May 27, 1856.

Rappinger, Caspar: Germany. 1st papers -
October 6, 1856 - Court of Common Pleas,
Lancaster County, Pennsylvania. 15/353: final
papers - August 5, 1872.

Rattigan, James: Ireland. S/176: final papers
- November 10, 1856.

Rattigan, Michael: Great Britain & Ireland.
1st papers - November 10, 1858 - Greenup Circuit
Court (not found). T/591: final papers -
November 20, 1858.

Regle, George: Beiern (Beren). 1st papers -
November 5, 1858 - Greenup Circuit (not found).
12/128: final papers - November 5, 1860.

Reinback (Rineback), Henry: Prusia. S/483:
1st July 21, 1857. 12/88: final papers -
July 27, 1860.

Reimlinger, George: Bavaria, Germany. 1st
papers - August 23, 1858 - Greenup Circuit
(not found). 12/321: final papers - August
1, 1862.

Reimlinger, George: Bavaria, Germany. 1st
papers - (date not given) - Greenup Circuit
(not found). 12/95: final papers - August
7, 1860.

Rendant, William: Germany. 1st papers - March
3, 1873 - place not given. 16/266: final
papers - August 3, 1876.

Riedel, Francis: Baden, Germany. 1st papers
September 11, 18___, Criminal Court of Baldimore
(sic). U/196: final papers - July 18, 1859.

Riely, John: Great Britain and Ireland. 1st
papers - September 2, 1856 - before the Clerk
of the Circuit Court of the United States for
the Western District of Pennsylvania. 12/32:
final papers - April 2, 1860.

Riley, Hugh: Great Britain. 1st papers -
August 18, 1845 - Circuit Court of Cole County,
Missouri. P/85: final papers - October 23,
1848.

Roberts, Edward J.: Great Britain. U/112: 1st papers - May 20, 1859.

Roberts, Thomas: South Wales. 26/59: 1st papers - March 12, 1870. Came to the United States on the 9th day of May, 1857, from the Aberdale Genmargunshire South Wales.

Roberts, Thomas G.: Great Britain. 1st papers - July 16, 1860 - place not given. 15/187: final papers - January 2, 1871.

Rohmann, John: Baden, Germany. 1st papers - March 22, 1858 - Probate Court, Hamilton County, Ohio. 12/43: final papers - May 2, 1860.

Rosse, Gustin: Switzerland. 12/320: 1st and final papers - July 29, 1862. Gustin Rosse states that he came to the United States on or about the 12th day of April 1852 from the County Seat of Delemont State of Berne in Switzerland; that he was under the age of 18 years when he came to the United States; has resided in the United States 3 years last preceding his arriving at the age of 21 years and has continued to reside therein until the present time.

Rosser, Isaac: England. 15/122: 1st and final papers - July 5, 1870. Came to United States a minor under age 21.

Sack, August: Germany. 16/289: 1st and final papers - November 6, 1876. Came to United States as a minor under the age of 21 years.

Schilling, Allent: Germany. 18/245: 1st and final papers - June 11, 1890. Came to United States a minor under the age of 18 years.

Schipp, John: Hessen. 1st papers - June 1840 - County Court of Ohio County, Virginia. P/84-5: final papers - October 23, 1848. NOTE: Entry recorded twice: once on P/84 and again on P/85.

Schneider, John: Damstadt, Germany. 1st papers - July 15, 1859 - Court of Common Pleas,

Hamilton County, Ohio. W/324: final papers -
July 20, 1863.

Seyfort, R.: Waldeck, Germany. 16/350: 1st
and final papers - September 26, 1877. Came
to United States as a minor under the age of
21 years.

Senate, Thomas: Great Britain and Ireland.
1st papers - April ____, 18____, Circuit Court
of Carter County, Kentucky. T/478: final
papers - November 9, 1858.

Shesler, Wolf: Bavaria, Germany. S/226: 1st
papers - November 17, 1856.

Shraub, John: Hesse Cassell, Germany. X/198:
1st and final papers - September 6, 1864. "On
the 2nd day of August 1861 I enlisted in the
volunteer army of the United States in War
of the Rebellion of 1861 and I was honorably
discharged on the 17th day of August 1864 from
the said military service after a service of
over three years in said military service.
That I was a native and subject of Hesse Cassell
in the Confederation of Germany; that I make
this application to be admitted to the rights
of a citizen of the United States, renouncing
all rights of citizenship to his native country,
and all allegiance thereof, and all titles
of nobility. (signed) John Shraub
     Sworn before me this Sixth day of September
A.D. 1864 before me Clerk of said Court by
John Schraub. (signed) Wm. Corum - G.C.C.
(Greenup Circuit Clerk).
     It appearing to the satisfaction of the
court that said John Shraub enlisted in the
army of the United States on the 2nd day of
August 1861 as a private in the Company commanded by J. N. Gilruth in the 27th Regiment of
Ohio infantry for three years and honorably
discharged on the 18th day of August 1864 as
appears from his discharge which was presented
to the court."

Slemme, Christian: Hanover, Germany. 1st
papers - July 21, 1856 - Greenup Circuit Court
(not found). U/588: final papers - May 25,
1860.

Smith, Christian: Grand Duchy of Baden, Kingdom of Prussia. 12/345: 1st and final papers - July 2, 1872. Came to United States as a minor under 21 years of age.

Smith, Frank: Ireland. 1st papers - August 2, 1873 - place not given. 16/266: final papers - August 3, 1876.

Smith, Henry: Bavaria, Germany. S/72: final papers - May 26, 1856.

Smith, John: Germany. 1st papers - October 9, 1848 - Common Pleas Court of Alleghany County, Pennsylvania. Q/65: final papers - October 19, 1851.

Smutz, John: Badan, Germany. Q/636: 1st papers - May 26, 1854. Came to United States October 24, 1850 from the Grand Duchy of Baden in Germany. S/269: final papers - November 22, 1856.

Snider, George: Bavaria, Germany. 1st papers - June 26, 1854 - Court of Common Pleas, Scioto County, Ohio. 12/96: final papers - August 7, 1860.

Steckler, Frederick: Hanover, Germany. 1st papers - July 19, 1858 - Greenup Circuit Court (not found). 12/90: final papers - August 3, 1860.

Steel, Alexander: Great Britain. 1st papers - October 12, 1852 - Court of Common Pleas, Scioto County, Ohio. U/232: final papers - July 21, 1859.

Steel, John: Great Britain and Ireland. R/222: final papers - May 22, 1855.

Steel, Robert: Great Britain and Ireland. R/221: 1st papers - May 22, 1855. Came to United States August 1851. U/232: final papers - July 21, 1859.

Stover, Julius: Germany. 17/190: 1st papers - November 3, 1884.

Sullivan, Daniel: Ireland. 18/152: 1st and
final papers - October 13, 1888. Native of
County of Cork, Ireland, came to United States
July 20, 1851; "on the ____ day of September
1862 he enlisted in the volunteer forces of
the armies of the United States of America
and served therein for a period of two years
and was honorably discharged therefrom."

Sweany, Edward: Britain. S/416: final papers
- May 23, 1857.

Sweany, Patrick: Britain. 1st papers -
December 21, 1850 - place not given. S/387:
final papers - May 20, 1857.

Teirney, John: Britain. 1st papers - August
15, 18____, Court of Common Pleas, Lawrence
County, Ohio. U/387: final papers - November
26, 1859.

Thom, Nicholas Fisher: Staffordshire, England.
M/191: 1st and final papers - July 6, 1840.
Born in County of Staffordshire, England; about
24 years of age; has been 7 years in United
States of America; about 5' 8 1/2" high, hazel
eyes, dark hair, light complexion and thin
visage.

Thomas, David D.: Great Britain. 1st papers -
February 25, 1857 - Court of Common Pleas
Lawrence County, Ohio. U/197: final papers -
July 18, 1859.

Thomas, Reece (Reis) P.: Wales. R/420: 1st
papers - November 19, 1855. Came to United
States March 27, 1848 from Wales. U/197: final
papers - July 18, 1859.

Thomer, Charles: Hassandamstead (sic), Germany.
S/491: 1st and final papers - July 22, 1857.
Came to U.S. 1846 under the age of 15.

Tillsley, William: England. P/183: 1st papers
- April 25, 1849. Came to U.S. October 1847
and landed at New York; 39 years of age and
has the following children: (ages as of April
25, 1849). Mary Ann (18); Samuel (16); Hubert

(14); Emma (12); Henry (10); William (8); Arthur
(6); Sarah (4); and the only child born in
U.S., James (1). Q/534: final papers - May
16, 1854.

Timmeny (Timany), Anthony: Great Britain.
P/450: 1st papers - April 30, 1851. Q/534:
final papers - May 16, 1854.

Tobin, Patrick: Ireland. S/198: final papers -
November 13, 1856.
Vahrson (Vohrson), John: Prussia (Preosen).
T/315: 1st papers - May 21, 1858 (signed May
20, 1858, as Jahnn Vahrson). Aged 38 years,
5' 6" tall; grey eyes; spare made; 140 lbs;
dark brown hair. U/589: final papers - May
25, 1860.

Vohrson, Henry: Prussia. 1st papers - May
25, 1858. U/589: final papers - May 25, 1860.
See NOTE under John Henry Varhson

Vorhson (Varhson), John Henry: Poeysen (sic).
T/362: 1st papers - May 25, 1858 (signed May
24, 1858). 5'8" tall, 26 years old, brown
hair, hazel eyes, 161 lbs. NOTE: Could John
Henry Varhson and Henry Vohrson be the same
person? No papers were filed on May 25, 1858
for Henry Vohrson, but were filed on this date
for John Henry Varhson.

Varley, Joseph: Great Britain and Ireland.
1st papers - March 25, 1858 - Common Pleas
Court of Lawrence County, Ohio. 12/32: final
papers - April 2, 1860.

Waddell, Edwin Maitland: England. 15/26:
1st papers - July 17, 1869. Came to United
States September 13, 1867 from the Kingdom
of Great Britain. 15/377: final papers -
November 4, 1872.

Wagner, Henry: Germany. 18/154: 1st and
final papers - November 5, 1888.

Wagner, John: Baden, Germany. 1st papers -
January 3, 1859 - Common Pleas Court of

Hamilton County, Ohio. 15/129: final papers -
July 18, 1870.

Walezak, Lewis: Germany. 16/400: 1st papers -
April 17, 1878. Came to United States August
21, 1873 from __?__ nrnig in Germany.

Walker, Henry: Hanover, Germany. T/315: 1st
papers - May 21, 1858 (signed May 20, 1858).
Of medium size, light complexion, grey eyes,
thin and light brown hair, 162 lbs. 12/77:
final papers - June 25, 1860.

Walker, Thomas: Great Britain & Ireland. 1st
papers - May 2, 1850 - District Court of the
United States for the District of Delaware.
Q/520: final papers - May 15, 1854.

Wallbright, Christian F.: Germany. 7/156:
1st and final papers - September 5, 1842.
Resided in the United States 3 years next preceding his arriving at the age 21 and has continued to reside therein to the present time

Walley, John: Great Britain and Ireland.
R/130: final papers - November 27, 1854.

Waltemath, William: Germany. 1st papers -
May 19, 1856 - Greenup Circuit Court (not
found). T/407: final papers - July 19, 1858.

Walter, Emanuel: Wurtemburg, Germany. 12/43:
1st and final papers - May 2, 1860. Came to
United States in 1852; under age of 18 at time
of arrival; has resided in Greenup County for
the last 5 years.

Walther, Phillip: Germany. 1st papers - May
8, 1871 - Greenup Circuit Court (not found).
15/468: final papers - August 2, 1873.

Walezak, Lewis: Journig, Germany. 1st papers -
April 17, 1878 - (place not given). 17/107:
final papers - August 23, 1881.

Weidenhiller, George: Bavaria. 1st papers -
October 6, 1856 - Greenup Circuit Court (not
found). 12/91: Final papers - August 3, 1860.

Weitseytcousky, George: Germany. 1st papers - December 13, 1880 - (place not given). 17/161 - final papers - July 2, 1883.

Welch, Thomas: Great Britain & Ireland. Q/602: final papers - May 24, 1854.

Welch, Walter: England. 0/191: 1st papers - October 10, 1845 (signed October 9, 1845). 0/450: final papers - October 29, 1847.

Wella, Henry: Hanover, Germany. 1st papers - July 10, 1854 - Court of Common Pleas, Lawrence County, Ohio. T/416: final papers - July 19, 1858.

Wese, Adam: Germany. 1st papers - July 31, 1869 - Greenup Circuit (not found). 15/351: final papers - August 3, 1872.

Williams, David: Wales. 1st papers - November 7, 1864 - Greenup County Court (not found). 15/101: final papers - April 4, 1870.

Willink, Abraham: Holland. P/142: 1st papers - October 27, 1848. About 32 years old, of light complexion, brown hair, about 5 1/2 ft. high, hazel eyes and light proportioned. Q/243: final papers - July 23, 1852.

Willink, Berend William: Holland. 1st papers - August 25, 1858 - Greenup Circuit (not found). 12/150: Final papers - January 7, 1861.

Willink, Mannis (Manis): Holland. P/142: 1st papers - October 27, 1848. 5 1/2 ft. high, 42 years old, of light complexion, hazel eyes, brown hair and well proportioned. Q/53: final papers - November 15, 1851.

Wilson, James: England. 15/26: 1st and final papers - July 17, 1869. Came to United States as a minor under age of 21.

Wood, William: Great Britain and Ireland. R/131: final papers - November 27, 1854.

Zuchars, Alfred: Prussia. 1st papers - October 22, 1860 - Court of Common Pleas, Scioto County, Ohio. X/399: final papers - July 24, 1865.

Zuchars, Theodore: Prussia. 1st papers - August 2, 1860 - Court of Common Pleas for the City and County of New York. X/400: final papers - July 24, 1865.

Zuchars, William: Prussia. 1st papers - August 2, 1860 - Court of Common Pleas for the City and County of New York. X/399: final papers - July 24, 1865.

REVOLUTIONARY WAR PENSIONS
(and a few others)

Alexander, John: D/257 - July 30, 1818.
"Ordered that it be certified to the Secretary
of War and to all whom it may concern that
it is proved to the satisfaction of this court
that John Alexander, Greenup, Betsy, Peyton
and Lewis Alexander are under 16 years of age
and are the children and only heirs at law
of John Alexander dec'd late a private soldier
in the 17th Regiment of United States infantry."

Burns, Jeremiah: F/85 - April 25, 1821
(age 69).
"Schedule, District of Kentucky, Greenup
County and Circuit SCT: On this 25th day of
April 1821, personally appeared in open court,
being a court of record made so by statute
for the said Circuit and County aforesaid,
Jeremiah Burns, aged 69 years in October next,
resident in Greenup, who being first duly sworn
according to law doth on his oath declare that
he served in the Revoluntionary War as follows:
that he served in the Company, Regiment and
line as set forth in his original Declaration
and as stated in the certificate now sent,
and I do solemnly swear that I was a resident
citizen of the United States on the 18th day
of March, 1818, and that I have not since that
time by gift, sale or in any manner disposed
of my property or any parts thereof with intent
thereby so to diminish it as to bring myself
within the provisions of an Act of Congress
entitled, 'An Act to provide for certain persons
engaged in the Revolutionary War,' passed on
the 18th day of March, 1818, and that I have
not, nor has any person in trust for me, any
property or security, contracts or debts due
to me, nor have I any income other than what
is contained in the Schedule hereto annexed
and by me subscribed. (signed) Jeremiah Burns.
Jeremiah Burns states that he has no lands
nor negroes and that the following is his personal estate, to-wit: 3 cows and 5 calves
worth $38.00, 1 horse beast worth $30.00, 1
rifle gun old worth $10.00, 11 head sheep and

lambs, worth $17.00, 3 hogs worth $5.00, knives and forks, plates and dishes worth $3.00, 1 old table and 3 chairs worth $1.00, 1 stove kettle, 1 little oven and skillet worth $2.50. This is all his property except bedding and furniture. He says that he has a wife 50 years old and very infirm and children living with him--3 sons, 11 years, 9 years, 27 years of age, 3 daughters 16, 14, and 5 years of age; he says he is not able to do a day's work, the rim of his belly having been broke and is by occupation a farmer. (signed) Jeremiah Burns.

Sworn to and declared on the 25th day of April 1821 before me, Eli Shortridge, Circuit Judge of the 11th Judicial District for the State of Kentucky, in open Court. Given under my hand this day above written. (signed) E. Shortridge, Circuit Judge.

Ordered that it be certified to the Secretary of War that Jeremiah Burns personally came into open court, the same being a court of record made so by Statute and also being so from its general jurisdiction and from its having power to fine and imprison, and made oath to the foregoing Declaration and Statement, and also made oath and subscribed to the Schedule of his property thereto annexed, and it is further certified that it is the opinion of the Judge that the said Schedule is a correct one and that the prices thereto annexed are reasonable."

Bush, John: F/11 - October 24, 1820 (age 67).
"John Bush came into court and made oath to the following Declaration and Statement, to-wit: State of Kentucky, Greenup County, SCT: John Bush states that he is aged 68 years on the 20 December next, and he makes the following Declaration and Statement in order to obtain the pension allowed by law to Revolutionary soldiers, viz: that he was drafted a private in Culpepper County, Virginia, some time prior to the Declaration of Independence, for 18 months, Capt. Killpatrick and Col. Christian Begger of Virginia and served out the term and was discharged at Cumberland old courthouse Virginia at the end of the time

by Capt. Killpatrick and that said Department
War on the Continental Establishment, and that
he served on the Continental Establishment
against the common enemy. That he lost his
discharge and has no evidence of his service
in his power other than his statement and reference to the record of the War Department. That
the following is a schedule of his property,
to-wit: he has no land, nor negroes, no horses,
sheep or any other property than what follows:
3 horses value $80, 3 cows and a calf and one
yearling $36, 28 hogs $30, 2 beds and furniture.
That he has parted with no property since the
passage of the law of any kind, and that he
has a wife aged 64 years. That he is in reduced
circumstances and stands in need of the pension
allowed him by law for a support.
    I, Eli Shortridge, Circuit Judge for the
11th Judicial District composed of the counties
of Bath, Greenup, Montgomery, and Floyd, do
certify that the above Declaration was duly
made and sworn to before me, and that it appears
to my satisfaction that the said John Bush
is in indigent and reduced circumstances and
needs the assistance of his Country. Given
under my hand and seal this 23rd day of October
1820. (signed) Eli Shortridge, Circuit Judge.
    Ordered that it be certifed to the Secretary
of War that John Bush came personally into
open court, the same being a court of record
made so by statute and also from its general
jurisdiction and from its having power to fine
and imprison, and made oath to the foregoing
Declaration and Statement and also made oath
to the Schedule of his property thereunto
annexed, and it is further certified that it
is the opinion of the Judge that the said
Schedule is a correct one, and that the prices
thereto annexed are reasonable."

Dailey, James: F/5 October 24, 1820.
    "On motion of Elizabeth Dailey, Be it known
to the Secretary of War and all whom it may
concern that James Dailey, late a private
soldier of Captain Collins Company 26 Regiment
United States Infantry, was lawfully married
to Elizabeth Dailey, late Elizabeth Harson
and that they had one child living at the death

of said Daily, namely Vincent Daily, who is
the only heir at law of said James Daily,
deceased, all which is proven to the satisfaction of the Court and ordered to be certified
to the Secretary of War."

Dortch (Dorch), William: F/6 - October 24,
1820 (age 60).
    "William Dorch came into Court and made oath
to the following Statement and Declaration,
to-wit: State of Kentucky, Greenup County
SCT: On this 24th day of October 1820 personally appeared William Dorch in open court,
the same being a court of record for the Circuit
and County of Greenup, aged about 60 years,
resident in said County and Circuit of Greenup,
who being first duly sworn deposeth and saith
and on his oath doth declare that he served
in the Revolutionary War as follows: He
enlisted as a regular soldier in the beginning
of the year 1780.   He was enlisted by the Ensign
David Lucket on Roan Oak River in Virginia,
County of Mecklinburg, for 3 years and was
placed in the Company commanded by Capt.
Mitchell, which was a company of first Maryland
Regiment commanded by Col. Otha Holland Williams
and was then marched to the state of South
Carolina.   He was in Gates defeat about six
miles from Camden, and he was next at the
victory obtained by Col. Morgan over Farlton
at the Cowpens, and continued in the service
3 years three months and was discharged by
Gen. Smallwood at Annapolis in the State of
Maryland, and he has not retained his discharge.
He further states that he made his original
declaration on the 22 day of July 1818 and
has received a pension, the Certificate of
which is dated the 5th day June, 1819, No.
11362, inscribed on the Pension list roll of
the Kentucky Agency, and he doth solemnly swear
that he was resident citizen of the United
States on the 18th day of March 1818, and that
he has not since that time by gift or sale
or in any manner disposed of his property or
any part thereof with intent thereby to diminish
it so as to bring himself within the provisions
of an Act of Congress for certain persons
engaged in the land and naval service of the

United States in the Revolutionary War, passed
on the 18th day of March 1818, and that he
has not, nor any person in trust for him, any
property or securities contracts or debts due
to him nor any income other that what is contained in the Schedule hereto annexed and
by him subscribed: 3 head of horses of the
value of $60, 2 cows and one calf of the value
of $25, 2 sows and ten pigs $10, one chair,
2 water buckets $1, one small bake oven and
one kettle $6, one pewter dish & 3 plates $1,
one plow and geer $6, one asc (ax) and 3 old
hoes $2.50 one pair double trees $1.50, 2
crocks, 1 ladle, 3 spoons, 4 knives and forks
$2.00, 4 tins 25 cents, debts due $3.75. He
owes debts as follows, To Bibbs $5, to Hare
$1.25, John Montgomery $1.00. (signed) William
Dortch.
    He is by occupation a farmer, he is able
to work but a part of the time, having received
a wound at the Eulair Springs by a thrust of
a bayonnet, and is now much subject to pain
in his limbs and body. His family consists
at present of his wife and a weakly son of
15 years age. He has 10 children, but all
the rest have left him.
    Ordered that it be certified to the Secretary
of War that William Dorch came personally into
court, the same being a court of record made
so by Statute and also being so from its general
jurisdication and from its having power to
fine and imprison, and made oath to the foregoing Declaration and Statement, and also made
oath and subscribed to the Schedule of his
property thereunto annexed, and it is further
certified that it is the opinion of the Judge
that the said Schedule is a correct one and
that the prices thereto annexed are reasonable."

F/70 - April 23, 1821 (age 60)
    "Original Claim, District of Kentucky, Circuit
& County of Greenup, SCT: On this 23rd day
of April 1821 personally appeared in open court,
being a court of Record, to-wit: the Circuit
Court for said County, William Dorch, aged
about 60 years who being first duly sworn
according to law doth on his oath make the
following Declaration in order to obtain the

provisions made by the Acts of Congress of
the 18th March 1818 and the 1st May, 1820,
that he, the said William Dorch, enlisted for
the term of three years on the _____ day of
Jany., Feby. or March in the year 1780 in the
State of Virginia in the Company commanded
by Captain Mitchell in the Regiment commanded
by Colonel O. H. Williams in the line of the
State of Maryland on the Continental Establishment. That he continued to serve in the said
Corps until about August 1783, when he was
discharged from the said service in Annapolis
in the State of Maryland by General Smallwood.
That he was in the battles of the Cowpens and
Gates Defeat, and that he has no other evidence
now in his power of his said services except
that which was formerly sent and that which
is now enclosed, and in pursuance of the Act
of the 1st May 1820, I do solemnly swear that
I was a resident citizen of the United States
on the 18th day of March 1818, and that I have
not since that time by gift, sale or in any
manner disposed of my property or any part
thereof with intent thereby so to diminish
it as to bring myself within the provisions
of the Act of Congress entitled 'An Act to
provide for certain persons engaged in the
land and naval service of the United States
in the Revolutionary War,' passed on the 18th
day of March 1818, and that I have not, nor
has any person in trust for me, any property
or securities, contracts or debts due to me,
nor have I any income other than what is contained in the Schedule hereto annexed and by
me subscribed. William Dorch states that he
is a farmer, and that he has no land of his
own nor negroes, that he has a wife about 61
or 62 years of age and not able to do much
work, also one son about 16 years old and small
for his age, and that the following is all
the property he owns, to-wit: 3 head of horses
of the value of $50, 2 cows and 2 calves $25,
2 sows and ten pigs $10, 1 chair and two water
buckets $1, 1 small bake oven and one kettle
$6, 1 pewer (sic) dish and 3 plates $1, 1 plow
and gear $6, 1 axe and 3 old hoes $2.50, 1
pair double trees $1.50, two crocks, 1 table,
3 spoons, & 4 knives and forks $2, 4 tins $0.25,

debts due him $3.75, and he owes debts as
follows: To I. Gibbs $5, I. Hare $1.25, Jno.
Montgomery $1, and he says he is not able to
do a day's work and is failing in his ability
to labor and is subject to pain in his limbs
and body, that he received a wound at Eutan
Springs. (signed) Wm. Dorch. (by his mark)
   Ordered that it be certified to the Secretary
of War that William Dorch came personally into
open court, the same being a court of record
made so by Statute and also from its general
jurisdiction and from its having power to fine
and imprison, and made oath to the foregoing
Declaration and Schedule of his property thereto
annexed, and it is further certified that it
is the opinion of the Judge that the said Schedule is a correct one and that the prices thereto
annexed are reasonable."

Gholson, William: 7/236 - May 6, 1844.
   "Satisfactory proof was this 6th day of May,
1844 made in open court by the oath of Henry
A. Mead and Joseph Rigg that William Gholson
departed this life on the 14th day of September
1843 in the County of Greenup, State of
Kentucky, and that he was the identical person
who made an application for a pension, and
that said William Gholson left no widow, but
there are three children living whose names
are Elizabeth Rigg, James H. Gholson and Cynthia
Gholson.   James H. Gholson resides in the County
of Lawrence, State of Ohio, and Elizabeth Rigg
and Cynthia Gholson reside in the County of
Greenup, Kentucky."

Harsin, Garret: F/5 - October 24, 1820
(age 66).
   "Garret Harson came into court and made oath
to the following, viz, Declaration and Statement, to-wit: State of Kentucky, Greenup
County, SCT: Garret Harsin states that he
is a citizen of the County and State aforesaid,
and is aged 66 years on the 15th day of June
last, and he makes the following Declaration
and Statement in order to obtain the Pension
allowed by law to Revolutionary soldiers, viz:
That he enlisted as a sailor on board a Guard
ship on the north river at West Point some

time after the Declaration of Independence.
The ship was called the Hudson Sloop of War.
Capt. John Palmer for 18 months, and served
that time on said sloop of war, after which
he enlisted the Quartermaster General Department
as an artificer under Capt. John Parcels and
Col. Hughes of the State of New York.   That
he enlisted the Department of Fishkill for
3 years and served out the time, and was discharged at Fishkill at the end of the time
by Capt. John Parcels and said Department of
War on the Continental Establishment, and that
he served in both instances on the Continental
Establishment against the common enemy.   That
he has lost his discharge and has no evidence
of his services in his power other than his
statement and references to the records of
the War Department.   That the following is
a schedule of his property, to-wit: He has
what follows, 12 hogs value $18, 4 head of
cattle $20, 2 beds and furniture $16, amounting
to $54.   Note all his household and kitchen
furniture except waring (sic) apparel is valued
at $48.   That he has parted with no property
of any kind and that he has a wife aged 55
or 56 and son living with him aged 14 and 3
daughters.   That he is in reduced circumstances
and stands in need of the pension allowed him
by law for support.   (signed) Garret Harsin.
     I, Eli Shortridge, Circuit Judge for the
11th Judicial District, composed of the counties
of Bath, Montgomery, Greenup and Floyd, do
certify that the above Declaration and Statement
was sworn to before me by the said Garret
Harsin, and he further deposed he has no
witness, nor did he know of any within this
county, by whom he could prove his services
as stated in his Declaration and Statement.
From his statement I only certify his services.
I further certify it fully appeared to my satisfaction that he is in indigent circumstances
and needs the assistance of his Country.   Given
under my hand and seal this 23rd day of October,
1820.   (signed) E. Shortridge, Circuit Judge.
     Ordered that it be certified to the Secretary
of War that Garret Harson came personally into
open court, the same being a Court of record
made so by Statute and also being so from its

general instruction and from its having power
to fine and imprison, and made oath to the
foregoing Declaration and Statement and also
made oath and subscribed to the Schedule of
his property thereunto annexed, and it is further certified that it is the opinion of the
Judge that the said Schedule is a correct one
and that the prices thereto annexed are reasonable."

F/81 - April 24, 1821 (age 67).
  "Original Claim, District of Kentucky Circuit
and County of Greenup, SCT: On this 24th day
of April 1821, personally appeared in open
court, (a) being a court of record for the
County of Greenup and State of Kentucky, Garrett
Harsin aged 67 years who being first duly sworn
according to law, doth on his oath make the
following Declaration in order to obtain the
provision made by the Acts of Congress of the
18th of March 1818 and the 1st May 1820, and
that he, the said G. Harsin, enlisted for the
term of 3 years on the ____ day of _____ in
the year 1779 or 1780 in the state of New York
in the Company commanded by Capt. Parcels in
the company commanded by Col. Hughes in the
line of the State of New York, on the Continental Establishment, that he continued to serve
in said corps until his term was out when he
was discharged from said service in _____
in the state of New York at Fishkill by Capt.
John Parcels. That he was in the corps of
artificers and went with the army in that corps,
and that he has no other evidence now in his
power of his said services except what is sent,
and in pursuance of the Act of 1st May 1820,
I do solemnly swear that I was a resident
citizen of the United States on the 18th day
of March 1818, and that I have not since that
time by gift, sale or in any manner disposed
of my property or any part thereof with intent
thereby to diminish it as to bring myself within
the provisions of an Act of Congress entitled,
'An Act to provide for certain persons engaged
in the land and naval service of the United
States in the Revolutionary War,' passed on
the 18th day of April 1818, and that I have
not, nor has any person in trust for me, any

property or securities, contracts or debts
other than what is contained in the Schedule
hereto annexed and by me subscribed. Sworn
to and declared on the 24th day of April 1821
before me the Circuit Judge of said Court.
(signed) E. Shortridge.

Said Harsin states that soon after Burgoines
defeat in 1777 he enlisted for 18 months on
board a ten gun privateer called the Hutson
at Fishkill landing New York, Capt. John Palmer,
and served out said time and was discharged
by Capt. Palmer in 1779, and afterwards enlisted
under Capt. Parcels as before stated. The
following is a Schedule of his estate, towit: He owns no land or negroes and has 1
cow and 1 steer two years old value $20, 1
pot and one broken bake oven $1, 6 chairs with
wooden bottoms $2, 2 axes and one plow $5,
1 broken salt kettle $2, 4 pewter plates and
small earthen plates $2, 4 cups and tin saucers
and 3 pepper boxes $1, 1 coffee pot 75 cents,
and 6 knives and forks 50 cents, total $37.25
He has no other, except clothes and bedding,
and says that he had eight head of cattle more
last year, all of which died this last winter,
and he killed five hogs last winter for his
winter meat and for bacon. His wife is 58
and in a low state of health for many years
and nearly blind, and in fact is helpless and
unable to support herself by any sort of work.
He has 3 children with him, one is 16, one
18, and the other 15. The oldest is a boy
and the other two are girls and one of them
is defective in her eyes and not able to get
a living. (signed) Garrett Harsin.

Ordered that it be certified to the Secretary
of War that Garrett Harsin came personally
into open court, the same being a court of
record made so by statute and also being so
from its general jurisdiction and from its
having power to fine and imprison, and made
oath to the foregoing Declaration and Statement
and also made oath and subscribed to the
Schedule of his property, thereunto annexed,
and it is further certifed that it is the
opinion of the Judge that the said Schedule
is a correct one and that the prices thereto
annexed are reasonable."

Johnson, John: D/165 - April 27, 1818.
   "The affidavit of John Johnson being filed
and sworn to in open court, and it appearing
to the satisfaction of the court that said
John Johnson is in very poor and indigent
circumstances, it is, therefore, ordered that
the same be certified to the Secretary of the
War Department of the United States."

D/245 - July 29, 1818.
   "John Johnson came personally into court
and made oath to a declaration and statement
to enable him to obtain a pension under an
act of Congress as a Revolutionary soldier,
it is ordered to be certified to the Secretary
of War."

F/38 - October 30, 1820 (age 76).
   "John Johnson came into court this day and
made oath to the following Declaration and
Statement, to-wit: District of Kentucky, SCT:
On this 30th day of October 1820 personally
appeared in open court, being a court of record
made so by statute in and for the County and
Circuit of Greenup, John Johnson, aged 76 years,
resident in the County of Greenup in said County
who being first duly sworn according to law
doth on his oath declare that he served in
the Revolutionary War as follows: In the year
1777 he enlisted in the County of Harford in
the State of Conneticut for the term of 3 years
in the Company commanded by Capt. Henry Thompson
in the regiment commanded by Colonel Willis
in the line of the State of Conneticut, that
he continued to serve in the said corps for
3 years, when he was discharged from the said
service in the said County of Harford in the
State of Connecticut.   That he was in an engage-
ment with the Indians of Wyoming, that he has
heretofore received a pension, Certificate
No. 13443, in consequence of his original
declaration dated 29 July 1818.   And I do
solemnly swear that I was a resident of the
United States on the 18th day of March 1818,
and that I have not since that time by gift,
sale or in any manner disposed of any property
or any part thereof with intent thereby so
to diminish it as to bring myself within the
provisions of the Act of Congress entitled,

'An Act to provide for certain persons engaged
in the land and naval service of the United
States in the Revolutionary War,' passed on
the 18th day of March 1818, and that I have
not, nor has any person in trust for me, any
property or securities, contracts or debts
due to me, nor have I any income other than
is contained in the Schedule hereto annexed
and by me subscribed, to-wit: one cow and
calf worth $12, one heifer worth $9, one rifle
gun worth $4, and a note of $8 to be paid in
corn, he has no occupation by which he can
make a living, he has none of his family
residing with him except his wife, who is unabl
to render him any assistance from her infirm
state occasioned by old age. (signed) John
Johnson.

    Ordered that it be certified to the Secretar
of War that John Johnson came personally into
open court, the same being a court of record,
made so by statute and also being so from its
general jurisdiction and from its having power
to fine and imprison, and made oath to the
foregoing Declaration and Statement and made
oath and subscribed to the Schedule of his
property thereunto annexed, and it is further
certified that it is the opinion of the Court
that the said Schedule is a correct one, and
that the prices thereto annexed are reasonable.

F/80 - April 24, 1821 (age 77).
    "Schedule, District of Kentucky, Greenup
County and Circuit SCT: On this 23rd day of
April 1821, personally appeared in open court,
being a court of record for said Circuit and
County aforesaid, John Johnson aged 77 years
resident in Greenup aforesaid in said Circuit
Court or Corporation, who being first duly
sworn according to law doth on his oath declare
that he served in the Revolutionary War as
follows: That he served in the company, regiment and line as set forth in his Original
Declaration and as stated in the certificate
now sent, and I do solemnly swear (or affirm
as the case may be) that I was a resident
citizen of the United States on the 18th day
of March 1818, and that I have not since that
time by gift, sale or in any manner disposed

of any property or any part thereof with intent
thereby so to diminish it as to bring myself
within the provisions of the Act of Congress
entitled, 'An Act to provide for certain persons
engaged in the land and naval service of the
United States in the Revolutionary War,' passed
on the 18th day of March 1818, and that I have
not, nor has any person in trust for me, any
property or securities, contracts or debts
due to me, nor have I any income other than
what is contained in the Schedule hereto annexed
and by me subscribed. (signed) John Johnson.
(by his mark).

John Johnson states that he has no land
or negroes and that the following is his personal estate, viz: one cow and calf and one
heifer worth $21, 1 rifle gun very old $4,
3 plates and one watch $10, no hogs, sheep
or stock other than as above, and the same
was bought with his pension money heretofore
drawn. He has no home of his own and no child
with him, in fact he lives with a son who is
married, and is 50 years old. That his wife
is crazy for many years and that she is kept
confined at the son's house, and he has to
get a person to assist him in taking care of
her, he has no one to help him to do anything,
except for hire or charity, and is himself
affected with pains and rheumatic affections.
(signed) John Johnson.

Ordered that it be certified to the Secretary
of War that John Johnson came personally into
open court, the same being a court of record
made so by statute and also from its general
jurisdiction and being so from its having power
to fine and imprison, and made oath to the
foregoing Declaration and also made oath and
subscribed to the Schedule of property thereunto
annexed, and it is further certified that it
is the opinion of the Judge that the said
Schedule is a correct one and that the prices
thereto annexed are reasonable."

Lawson, James: I/49 - October 1, 1832.
"James Lawson, a soldier of the Revolution,
this day produced in Court his declaration
to obtain a pension under the Act of Assembly
of the 7th of June 1832, and subscribed and

sworn in open court, and also the Reverend
Charles Philips, a clergyman, and Clement H.
Waring, both citizens of this county, and subscribed and sworn to in their certificates
annexed to said Declaration, and the said court
do hereby declare their opinion, after the
investigation of the matter and after putting
the interrogatories prescribed by the War
Department, that the above named applicant
was a Revolutionary Soldier, and served as
he states, and the Court further certifying
that it appears to them that Charles Philips,
who has signed the annexed Certificate to said
Declaration, is a clergiman resident in the
County of Greenup, and that Clement H. Waring,
who has also signed the same, is also a residen*
of the County aforesaid and is a credible
person, and that their statement is entitled
to credit."

Love, John: D/165 - April 27, 1818.
   "The affidavit of John Love being filed and
sworn to in open court, and it appearing to
the satisfaction of the court that the said
John Love is in very poor and indigent circumstances, it is therefore, ordered that the
same be certified to the Secretary of the War
Department of the United States."

McGuire, Robert: D/257 - July 30, 1818.
   "Ordered that it be certified to the
Secretary of War and to all to whom it may
concern that it is proved to the satisfaction
of the court that John McGuire is the father
and only heir at law of Robert McGuire, late
a private soldier enlisted by Captain Charles
Quary into the 17th Regiment of United States
infantry."

Moore, Nathaniel H.: Eo/228 - July 29, 1819.
   "On the motion of Chloe S. Moore in open
court, be it known to the Secretary of War
and to Iasiah Meigs, Esquire, commissioner
of the Land Office, and to all others whom
it may concern, that on this day the said Chloe
S. Moore made satisfactory proof that she was
the wife (by lawful intermarriage) of Nathaniel

H. Moore, late a private in Captain ____ Company
of the ____ United States infantry and that
she produced the notification of Land Warrant
5632 under date 1st July 1816 and proved that
said Nathaniel H. Moore, to whom the said
issued, departed this life since the said 1st
day of July 1816, and that she is still his
widow and unmarried, and it is further certified that said Chloe S. Moore is a citizen
of this state, and that her husband died child-
less and intestate, and that by the laws of
this state the said Chloe S. Moore is entitled
to one-half of the real and personal estate
of said Nathaniel H. Moore, deceased, and his
father, John Moore, the other moiety."

Patton, James: I/48 - October 1, 1832.
  "James Patton, a soldier of the Revolution,
this day produced in court his Declaration
to obtain a pension under the Act of Congress
of the 7th of June 1832 and subscribed and
sworn to the same in open Court, and also the
Rev. Charles Philips, a Clergiman, and John
Culver, both citizens of this County, subscribed
and sworn to their certificate annexed to said
Declaration, and the said Court do hereby
declare their opinion, after the investigation
of the matter and after putting the interrogatories prescribed by the War Department, that
the above named applicant was a Revolutionary
soldier and served as he states, and the Court
further certifies that it appearing to them
that Charles Philips, who has signed the annexed
certificate to said Declaration, is a clergiman
resident in the County of Greenup, and that
John Culver, who has also signed the same,
is also a resident of the County aforesaid
and is a credible person, and that their statement is entitled to credit."

7/314 - March 2, 1846.
  "Be it remembered that John Culver and John
Poage came personally into Open Court and being
solemnly sworn proved that they were acquainted
with James Patton, formerly of this County,
and that they knew him for about twenty eight
years during which time he resided in this
County. That he died about the 1st day of

August, 1845, leaving John Patten his only
heir at law, to our knowledge being all he
left, and who is still living. They further
proved that the James Patton above named is
the one who has been drawing a pension as a
Revolutionary Soldier, the same is ordered
to be entered of record for the benefit of
all those whom it may concern."

Townsend, Jackson: 8/180 - September 3, 1849.
    "It is hereby certified that satisfactory
proof was this day made to this County Court
of Greenup County in the State of Kentucky
by the oath of Benjamin F. Mead and General
John Poage, who are persons entitled to a
credit, that Jackson Townsend is the Father
of that Jackson who volunteered to go to Mexico
during the war with Mexico and who was a private
soldier in the United States Service, and it
is further certified satisfactorally proven
by said witnesses that said Jackson never was
married and died leaving neither wife nor child
all which is ordered to be certified to the
pension office at Washington D.C.
    It is certified that this day Jackson Town-
send personally appeared in open court and
made declaration on oath that his son, Jackson
Townsend, enlisted during the War with Mexico
in the service of the United States on the
26th of August 1847 at Portsmouth, Ohio, and
marched for Mexico, and he belives and has
understood that he died at Vera Cruz in Mexico.
He further declares on oath that said Jackson
never was married and had no child or children
at the time of this death, and that said Jackson
Townsend was his son, which is ordered to be
certified."

Willis, Henry S.:   F/420 - October 13, 1823.
    "Be it known to the Secretary of War and
to all to whom it may concern that Henry S.
Willis, late a soldier in the army of the United
States, to whom Land Warrant No. 7601 was
issued, dated on the 14th day of December 1816,
departed this life since that date, and that
Joseph Willis is the brother and only heir
at law of said Henry S. Willis, deceased, which
facts being proven to the satisfaction of the
Court, the same are ordered to be certified."

Young, John: 7/169 - November 7, 1842.
  "On this 7th day of November 1842 personally
appeared before the County Court of the County
of Greenup, John Young, a resident of the County
of Greenup and State of Kentucky, aged 78 years
the 24th day of August last passed, who being
first duly sworn according to law, doth on
his oath make the following declaration in
order to obtain the benefit of the provision
made by the Act of Congress passed June 7,
1832.
  That he entered the service in the spring
of 1778 as a substitute for his Father, Reuben
Young, in Captain James Croncher (Crouchen)
Company and Colonel George Stubblefields ridge-
ment (sic) in the County of Spottsylvania,
State of Virginia. That they marched to Cobbs
Point to which the regiment rendesvoused (sic)
and remained and three weeks from thense (sic)
marched to Petersburg, where the regiment was
discharged, making a tour of 35 days, and then
he was enlisted in the United States Army on
the Virginia Continental line as a rider of
express from North to South. That he was
enlisted by Richard Young, who was Quartermaster
at Fredericksburg, in the month of August 1778.
That his wages was $12.50 per month by the
orders of Brig. Genl. George Weeden, who was
a general of the Continental Army and stationed
at Fredericksburg. That he was enlisted for
and during the War. When Genl. Weeden wanted
a draught of Malitia or supplies from the
following Counties, he would take him from
the regular rout (sic) and send him to the
Cols. of the Counties, viz, Spottsylvania,
Louisa, Albemarle, Augusta, Rockingham,
Shannondoe, Frederick, Hamshire, Berkley,
Orange, Stafford, King George, Westmoreland,
Richmond, Lancaster and Northumberland. That
he was kept constantly riding from North to
South except when taken off by Genl. Weeden
to convey an express to the Colonels of the
above named Counties. That a great part of
his services was performed in the night, and
he was frequently in great danger of being
taken by Col. Farltons light horse. That he
was sent to Little York with an express directed
to Col. Timothy Pickering, who was Quartermaster

Genl., and was detained their (sic) by Col.
Pickering until after the seige to carry expres
from one point of the army to the other. The
most of this service was performed in the night
That he saw Cornwallis surrender to Genl. Washington, and he was sent with the first intelli-
gence of the surrender of Cornwallis to the
North, and then he was kept in service as a
rider of express when it was necessary, and
the balance of his time was engaged in taking
care and collecting the public property until
the last of April 1782, and then he was discharged by Genl. George Weeden, which discharge
he has lost by reason of his coming to Ky the
fall after he received it. He states he served
35 days as militiaman and three years and eight
months as a rider of express in the Continental
service, making in all three years and nine
months that he was in the service.

He further states that there was not any
man rendered more service than he did, that
he was taken out of the rank and put as a rider
of express, which was much harder and more
dangerous, he was frequently in great danger
of being taken by the Brittish and had to be
exposed to all sorts of weather, was very near
freezing to death several times. That there
was no man whose service was of more importance
than his. That all the important communications
was intrusted (sic) to him. That he has frequently rode from Fredericksburg to Richmond
and back to Fredericksburg in twenty four hours
making 150 miles, bearing express from Genl.
Washington to Genl. Green and back to Genl.
Washington.

He further states that in the month of
September 1782 he came to Kentucky with Richard
Young, and then returned to Virginia in the
same winter and married his present wife on
the 12th day of March 1785, whose name was
Mary Moore, and then moved to Kentucky in the
fall of '87 and was in every expedition against
the indians that was after he got to Ky, was
with Genl. Wilkerson, Scott and Wayne's
campagnes. He hereby relinquishes his every
claim whatever to a pension or annuity except
the present, and he declares that he is not
on the Pension Roll of any agency in any State

or Territory of the U. States. (signed) John
Young.

Sworn to and subscribed the day and year
aforesaid, November 7th Amendment to the Declaration 1842. (signed) Jesse Corum.

He states that it is said that he was born
August 24, 1764, and entered the service in
his fourteenth year, and was married the 12th
of March '85, in his twenty first year, and
moved to Kentucky at the time stated above
and have lived in the above named state ever
since. (signed) John Young.

Sworn and subscribed the day and year aforesaid. (signed) Jesse Corum.

And the said Court do hereby declare their
opinion that the above named applicant was
a Revolutionary soldier, and served as he
states. (signed) Jesse Corum.

Zornes, Andrew: F/73 - April 24, 1821 (age
64).

"Schedule, District of Kentucky, Greenup
Circuit Court, on this 24th day of April 1821,
personally appeared in open Court, being a
Court of record for the said Circuit and County
of Greenup, Andrew Zornes, aged about 64 years,
resident in Greenup, Ky., in said Circuit Court,
who being first duly sworn according to law
doth on his oath declare that he served in
the Revolutionary War as follows: he enlisted
and served as stated in his Original Declaration herewith sent and was discharged at Pittsburg at the end of 3 years by Col. Bigers,
and I do solemly swear that I was a resident
citizen of the United States on the 18th day
of March 1818, and that I have not since that
time by gift, sale or in any manner disposed
of my property or any part thereof with intent
thereby so to diminish it as to bring myself
within the provisions of an act of Congress
entitled, 'An Act to provide for certain persons
engaged in the land and naval service of the
United States in the Revolutionary War,' passed
on the 18th day of March 1818, and that I have
not, nor has any person in trust for me, any
property or securities, contracts or debts
due to me, nor have I any income other than
what is contained in the Schedule hereto annexed

and by me subscribed, sworn to and declared
on the 24th day of April 1821 before me, the
Circuit Judge for the County aforesaid, the
same being a court of record. The Schedule
of Andrew Zornes declares and shows that he
has no real estate and no negroes and has the
following property, to-wit: 2 head of horses
of the value of $60, 4 cows $25, 4 yearling
calves and two small calves $18, 14 head of
hogs one year old $14, 17 head of sheep and
7 lambs $20, one rifle $15, 2 broken kettles
$1, 2 pots and one Dutch oven $3, 4 plates,
one dish and one bason (sic), all old $2, one
half dozen cups and saucers at 75 cents, three
or four old knives and forks worth nothing--
say 25 cents, 5 tin cups all old 25 cents,
total $159.25, and that he has no other property
except necessary bedding and clothing, he has
sold one cow to his son worth $10 in trade
or $7 in cash since the passage of the law.
That his wife is 57 years old and is helpless
since last Christmas. She has been unhealthy
all her life, two little girls living with
him, one 14 and the other 11 years old, the
last is sickly and not able to work, but the
oldest can do some work. That he is a labourer
by profession and is a squatter upon land,
and the owner may turn him out at pleasure.
He says he owes nothing except his taxes, and
has owing to him about $2.50. (signed) Andrew
Zornes (by his mark).
    Ordered that it be certified to the Secretary
of War that Andrew Zornes came personally into
open court, the same being a court of record
made so by statute and also being so from its
general jurisdication and from its having power
to fine and imprison, and made oath to the
foregoing Declaration and Statement and also
made oath and subscribed to the Schedule of
his property thereunto annexed, and it is further certified that it is the opinion of the
Judge that the said Schedule is a correct one,
and that the prices thereto annexed are reasonable."

F/274 - October 15, 1822 (age 66).
    "State of Kentucky, Greenup Circuit, 11th
Judicial District, SCT: Original Claim
Schedule:

On this 15th day of October 1822 personaly
(sic) appeared in open Court (this being a
Court of record by the laws of this state being
so adjudged by the other Tribunals of this
state with unlimited jurisdiction in point
of amount with power to fine and imprision,
always keeping a record of its proceedings)
Andrew Zornes aged about 66 years, a resident
within the Circuit aforesaid and County of
Greenup, who being first duly sworn according
to law, doth on his oath make the following
Declaration in order to obtain the provision
made by the Acts of Congress of the 18th of
March 1818 and the 1st of May 1820 that he,
the said Andrew Zornes, enlisted for the term
of 3 years sometime in the month of September
1776 at Monongahale near Morganstown in the
State of Virginia in the Company commanded
by Capt. John Wilson in the 8th Pennsylvania
Regiment commanded by Lt. Col. George Wilson,
and afterward commanded by Col. McCoy in the
line State of Pennsylvania on the Continental
Establishment, that he continued to serve in
the said Corps until September 1779, when he
was honorably discharged at Pittsburg in the
State of Pennsylvania, and that he was not
in any battles, and that he has no other
evidence now in his power of his said services
except of the Depositions of Ensign John Hargess
and Martin Zornes, which are hereto annexed
and submitted to the Honorable Secretary of
War, and the said Andrew Zornes further states
on oath that he made his Original Declaration
of his said services on the 24th day of April
1820, but has not yet received his pension
certificate, and in pursuance of the act of
the 1st of May 1820, I do solemnly swear that
I was a resident citizen of the United States
on the 18th day of March 1818, and that I have
not since that time by gift, sale or in any
manner disposed of my property or any part
thereof with intent thereby so to diminish
it as to bring myself within the provisions
of an act of Congress entitled, 'An Act to
provide for certain persons engaged in the
land and naval service of the United States
in the Revolutionary War,' passed on the 18th
day of March 1818, and that I have not, nor

has any person in trust for me, any property
or securities, contracts or debts due to me,
nor have I any income other than what is contained in the Schedule hereto annexed and by
me subscribed (viz) Two horse beasts, one old
horse @ $30 and mare @ $30, three cows of the
smallest kind of cattle @ $9 each in the sum
of $27, three young calves at $1.50 each is
$4.50, one heifer @ $6, two year-lambs @ $2.50
each is $5, 23 head of sheep at $20, one plow
$3 and other farming utensils, all valued at
$4.50, household furniture of every kind @
$5. I have been a squatter on Gen. Robert
Poage's land and that very poor land, which
has not yielded me any annual income, and shall
now be compelled to pay rent or be turned off
the land. I have no other property real or
personal, and the property as by me given in
amounts to the sum of $134. I have no other
family than myself, my wife, named Rebecca,
two children, named Sela and Delpha, the one
12 and the other 15 years of age. I am too
old to work, being very infirm, my wife is
58 years of age and sickly and unable to work,
and she is an expense to support, not being
able to support herself, my 2 daughters are
not able to contribute any support to their
mother and father, as they can scarcely support
themselves, being females and unable to labor
on the farm. Sworn to and Declared on the
15th day of October 1822 before Silas W.
Robbins, Circuit Judge of 11th Judicial
District. Subscribed by me. (signed) Andrew
Zornes.

Ordered that it be certified to the Secretary
of War that Andrew Zornes came personally into
open Court, the same being a Court of record
made so by statute and also being so from its
general jurisdiction and from its having power
to fine and imprison, and made oath to the
foregoing Declaration and Schedule which are
by him subscribed, and it is further certified
that it is the opinion of the Judge that the
said Schedule is a correct one and that the
prices thereto annexed are reasonable."

LUNACY INQUESTS

Lunacy Inquests were periodically held to determine if there had been a change in the "physical condition, circumstances or estate" of the individual before the Court and to authorize payment of the allowance for support for the previous year to the individual's committee. These inquests were held once a year--usually in the aniversary month of their original inquest. For the sake of brevity, I have not listed each inquest, unless there was a change noted, or it was the first or last entry found for that individual during this time period.

By the 1890's Lunacy Inquests no longer went into great detail in the record as they had in previous years. Entries during this time period usually stated only that "An inquest was this day held upon _____, an idiot (or lunatic) and filed." The record no longer gave all the information involved in determining whether they were of sound or unsound mind.

* * * * * *

Adkins, Barney:
37/491 - April 7, 1896.
"An inquest was this day held upon Barney Adkins, a lunatic, and recorded."

Adkins, Bennie:
38/61 - November 5, 1896.
"It appearing to the satisfaction of the court that Jennie Belle Smith, Mary Wheeler, and John Woods, lunatics, and George Wurts, Cordelia Caywood, Amos Carr, Cynthia A. Burton, Celia Leathers, Lucy Middaugh, Minnie McGinnis, Did Nicholls, Isaiah Stepter, Minta Traylor, John Traylor, Bennie Adkins, Gracie Guilkey, James A. Kitts, William C. Kitts, Bertha Traylor, and John Murphy, idiots, are still alive, in the care of their committees, and have not sufficient estate for their support, and that their parents are still unable to support them, it is ordered that the allowance

of $75.00 per annum for their support be con-
tinued from the last payment, and that the
same be copied and certified to the Auditor
for payment."

39/368 - November 7, 1901.
"It appearing to the satisfaction of the
Court that Gracie Guilkey, Hannah Davis, Ella
Jennings, Birdie Traylor, William C. Kitts,
James A. Kitts, Bennie Adkins, John Murphy,
and Martha Wadkins, idiots, are still alive,
in the care of their committees, and have not
sufficient estate for their support, and that
their parents are still unable to support them,
it is ordered that the allowance of $75.00
per annum each for their support be continued
from the last payment, and that the same be
copied and certified to the Auditor of Public
Accounts for payment."

Barber, Jacob:
I/312 - October 6, 1834 (age 20).
"On motion of the attorney for the Commonwealth, it is ordered that a jury de-idiota
inquirendo be summoned to inquire into the
estate and mind of Jacob Barber, and thereupon
the court appointed William H. Taylor as
attorney to defend said Barber, and said Barber
being in open court, the following jury being
empannelled (sic) and sworn to wit: William
H. Miranda, Stephen Powell, Andrew Flynn, Carter
Smiley, Barney Shipton, John Gallagher, Charles
Jackson, John Price, William Applegate, John
Gray, Edward Stephenson and John Osborne returned the following verdict, to wit: 'We the
Jury find Jacob Barber to be a lunatic and
that he has become so since the age of 10 years,
that he is now 20 years of age, and that he
has no estate out of which to support. This
Court appoints James Rouse as a committee to
take charge of said Barber.'"

Beckworth (Beckwith), Ben:
35/106 - August 26, 1885 (age 10).
"Upon motion of the Attorney for the Commonwealth it is ordered that a Writ of De Idiota
Inquirendo issue in the case of Ben Beckworth,
an idiot, returnable immediately, to inquire

into the state of mind of said Ben Beckworth, and it is ordered that Thomas N. Paynter be appointed counsel for the said Beckworth. Whereupon came a jury, to-wit: G. H. Callihan, W. F. Crump, Mason G. Burn, John Pratt, James H. Savage, Turner Crump, Samuel Hornbuckle, Asberry Ward, John Goad, Thomas A. Traylor, James F. Taylor and W. S. Withrow who being sworn according to law returned the following verdict, to-wit: 'We of the jury find from the evidence that Ben Beckworth is a person of unsound mind and an idiot; that the unsoundness of mind has existed from his birth; that he was born in Greenup County, and resides in Greenup, and is 10 years old; that he was not brought into this state for the purpose of becoming a charge upon the Commonwealth; that he owns no estate of any kind, that his father is dead and mother living and resides in Greenup County, Kentucky, and they (have) not estate sufficient to support the person under trial, and said Beckworth is not capable of laboring in whole or in part for his support.' (signed) William S. Withrow, foreman.

It is ordered that B. F. Brown be appointed a committee to take charge of said Ben Beckworth and provide him with suitable diet, clothing, etc., and that he be allowed therefor at the rate of $75.00 per annum from this date, to be paid upon further order of this Court. B. F. Brown, committee as aforesaid, appeared in Court, and with Thomas J. Wilson as his surety, who is accepted and approved, executed bond according to law."

36/4 - August 28, 1888.
"It appearing to the satisfaction of the Court that Ben Beckwith, an idiot, was alive and in the care of his committee up to the 25th day of May, 1888, when he died, and that he had no estate for his support, and that his parents were unable to support him. It is ordered that the allowance of $75.00 per annum be continued from the last payment to the day of his death, which is ordered to be copied and certified to the Auditor for payment for, and it is further ordered that said committee be allowed $5.00 for the necessary

expense of the burial of said Ben Beckwith."

Beckworth, Mariah:
35/236 - August 26, 1886.
   "It appearing to the satisfaction of the court that Jacob Steenrod, Grant Damarin, Did Nicholls, Mariah Beckworth, John Murphy and George Wurts are still alive, in the care of their committees, and have not estate sufficient for their support, and that their parents are unable to support them, it is ordered that the allowance of $75.00 per annum be continued from the last payment and the same is ordered to be copied and certified to the Auditor of Public Accounts."

Bevel, Scott:
37/171 - November 9, 1893.
   "An inquest was this day held upon Scott Bevel and recorded, and the Jury returned the following verdict: 'We the Jury find the defendant of sane mind.' (signed) Jeremiah Farmer, foreman."

Boyd, Mary Ann:
Z/382 - September 6, 1869.
   "It appearing to the satisfaction of the Court that Mary Ann Boyd, who was found to be an idiot by the Boyd Circuit Court at its December Special Term 1864, has removed to the County Greenup and is still alive and has not sufficient estate for her support, and that her parents are still unable to support her. It is ordered that Moses F. Dupuy be appointed a committee to take charge of said Mary Ann Boyd and provide her with suitable diet, clothing, etc. It is further ordered that said Moses F. Dupuy give bond and security for the faithful performance of his duty in this case, and the said Dupuy gave bond with Trevanian Bartlett as his security, according to this order, and the same was accepted and ordered to be certified to the Auditor. It is further ordered that the allowance of $50.00 per annum be continued from the last payment and the same is ordered to be certified to the Auditor."

26/156 - September 8, 1870 (age 31).

"Mary Ann Boyd, who was heretofore found
to be an idiot by an inquest of the Boyd Circuit
Court, appeared in court, and on motion of
the attorney for the Commonwealth, it is ordered
that a Writ of Deidota Inquirendo issue for
the purpose of inquiring into the state of
mind of the said Mary Ann Boyd, returnable
immediately, and it is ordered that L. W.
Andrews, Esq., be appointed council for the
said Mary Ann Boyd. Whereupon came the Jury,
Daniel C. Callihan, Robert Stewart, H. C. McCoy,
Sam Womack, Wm. A. Womack, John Riggs, H. I.
McAllister, George Gammon, Richard Morton,
George Howland, Jacob Howe and John Fuller,
who being sworn according to law returned the
following verdict, towit: 'We the jury find
that Mary Ann Boyd, whom we have in charge,
is of unsound mind and an idiot, and has been
destitute of mind from her birth, she was born
in Floyd County, Kentucky, and is now 31 years
of age. Her father is alive, but has no estate
sufficient for her support. He resides in
Greenup County. The said Mary Ann Boyd has
no estate of her own in possession, reversion
or remainder and is incapable of laboring in
whole or in part for her support. She has
heretofore, by a verdict of a jury and the
judgment of the Floyd (Boyd ?) Circuit Court,
been found an idiot, and since then there has
been no change in her mind, physical condition
or estate.

Wherefore it is adjudged by the court that
the said Mary Ann Boyd is an idiot, and that
it is ordered that Moses F. Dupuy be continued
as her committee, and that he be allowed at
the rate of $50.00 per annum for her support
from the last payment and that same be certified
to the Auditor."

28/159 - March 18, 1873.

"It appearing to the satisfaction of the
court that Mary Ann Boyd, an idiot, remained
in the care of her committee until the 15th
day of December, 1872, and was then removed
by her parents from the County of Greenup,
that during her continuance in said county
she had not sufficient estate for her support

and that her parents were unable to support
her, it is ordered that the allowance of $50.00
per annum be continued from the last payment
until said 15th day of December 1872, and that
the same be certified to the Auditor."

Brand, Jacob:
O/236 - April 28, 1846.
   "On motion of the attorney for the Commonwealth, it is ordered that the Sheriff of
Greenup County summon twelve housekeepers of
this county to appear here immediately to
inquire whether Jacob Brand, who is now in
open court, be or be not of sound mind, and
if he be not of sound mind, whether he was
so from the time of his birth or became so
afterwards, and what property he has; thereupon
came jury, towit: Matthew Warnock, Charles
Womack, John Culver, Lyman Collister, Levi
Hampton, James Nichols, Samuel Hardwick, Isaac
Bassett, Rezin Smith, Eli Cooper, Charles
Barrett, James Middaug, who being elected,
tried and sworn well and truly to inquire into
and ascertain the facts for which they were
summoned, and not being able to agree, it is
ordered that they be discharged."

Burchett, John:
Y/97 - March 12, 1866.
   "The following account was produced to the
Court by John Y. Wooldridge, viz: The Common-
wealth of Kentucky, to John Y. Wooldridge,

       taking John Burchett (who had
       been declared a lunatic by the
       Greenup County Court) from
       Greenupsburg, Greenup County,
       Kentucky to the Lunatic Asylum
       at Lexington, Kentucky, being 135
       miles to Covington, Kentucky, and
       98 miles to Lexington, Kentucky,
       making 233 miles, at 8 cents per
       mile each for self and one guard
       and lunatic...........................$55.92
       Ferrage at Covington, Kentucky...........40
       and 8 cents a mile each in the
       return from said asylum................37.28
              Total amount..................93.60
       Credit by Warrant from Dr. Chipley

```
                in Treasury........................30.00
                       Balance........................63.60
```

    Which said account amounting to the sum
of $63.60 was examined and allowed and ordered
to be filed and certified to the Superintendent
of the Eastern Lunatic Asylum. It appearing
to the court, upon an examination of the inquest
and upon proof introduced, that the lunatic
was delivered to the Keeper of the Lunatic
Asylum at Lexington, Kentucky, within six months
after the first attack of his lunacy."

Burriss, James:
38/209 - November 5, 1897.
    "It appearing to the satisfaction of the
court that Jennie Belle Smith, a lunatic,
William C. Kitts, James A. Kitts, Gracie
Guilkey, John Murphy, Birdie Traylor, Thomas
Hill, Bennie Adkins, James Burriss and Caroline
Ham, idiots, are still alive, in the care of
their committees, and have not sufficient estate
for their support, and that their parents are
still unable to support them, it is ordered
that the allowance of $75.00 per annum each
for their support be continued."

38/210 - November 5, 1897.
    "Ordered that John Reeves be removed as com-
mittee for James Burriss, an idiot, and that
William Messer be appointed committee for said
James Burriss in his place. He thereupon
appeared in Court and took the oath required
by law, and together with B. F. Reeves, Sr.
as his surety, who is accepted and approved
by the Court, executed bond to the Commonwealth of Kentucky as committee aforesaid,
conditioned according to law."

39/423 - April 9, 1902.
    "It appearing to the satisfaction of the
Court that James Burris, heretofore adjudged
to be an idiot by this Court, was alive in
the 9th day of April 1902, and had not sufficient estate for his support, and that his
parents were still unable to support him, and
that he was still in the care of his committee,
William Messer, and that at an inquest held

- 59 -

this day upon said James Burriss he was adjudged
to be a Harmless Lunatic, it is adjudged that
said William Messer be allowed at the rate
of $75.00 per annum for the support of said
James Burriss from the date of the last payment
until and including the 8th day of April 1902,
it is ordered to be copied and certified to
the Auditor of Public Accounts for payment."

Burton, Cynthia Ann:
35/153 - February 23, 1886 (age 50).
   "Upon motion of the attorney for the Commonwealth, it is ordered that a writ of de idota
inquirendo issue in the case of Cynthia A.
Burton, an idiot, returnable immediately, to
inquire into the state of mind of said Burton,
and it is ordered that Geo. T. Halbert, Esq.,
be appointed counsel for said Burton. Whereupon
came a jury, towit: J. G. Hern, Hamilton
Walker, S. H. Carnegy, Thomas Wilson, Arch
Conway, William Bradley, James Stark, Lewis
P. Harrison, William Loper, J. C. Bierly, Henry
Mead and James Cliften, who being duly sworn,
after hearing the evidence, returned the following verdict, viz: 'We the jury find from the
evidence that Cynthia A. Burton is a person
of unsound mind and an idiot; that the unsoundness of mind has existed from birth; that she
was born in Morgan County, Kentucky, and resides
in Greenup County, Kentucky, and is 50 years
old; that she was not brought into this state
for the purpose of becoming a charge upon the
Commonwealth; that she owns no estate of any
kind, that her father is living and mother
is living and reside in Greenup County,
Kentucky, and they have not estate sufficient
to support the person under trial, and said
Cynthia A. Burton is not capable of laboring
in whole or in part for her support.' (signed)
L. H. Carnegy, foreman"

35/197 - February 26, 1886.
   "Ordered that B. F. Brown be appointed a
committee to take charge of said Cynthia A.
Burton and provide her with suitable diet,
clothing, etc., and that he be allowed therefor
at the rate of $75.00 from date of finding
of the jury herein, to be paid upon the further

orders of this court, which is ordered to be
copied and certified to the Auditor."

37/440 - November 6, 1895.
"It appearing to the satisfaction of the
court that Cynthia Ann Burton, an idiot, is
still alive, in the care of her committee,
and has not sufficient estate for her support,
and that her parents are still unable to support
her, it is ordered that the allowance of $75.00
per annum for her support be continued from
the last payment and that the same be certified
to the Auditor for payment. Ordered J. Watt
Womack be appointed a committee for said Cynthia
Ann Burton in lieu of W. S. Warnock."

39/383 - November 11, 1901.
"It appearing to the satisfaction of the
court that Mary Wheeler and John Wood, lunatics,
and Amos Carr, Cynthia Ann Burton, Minta
Traylor, John Traylor, Lucy Middaugh, Did
Nicholls, Isaiah Stepter, Minnie McGinnis,
and Mary Griffith, idiots, are still alive,
in the care of their committees, and have not
estate sufficient for their support, and that
their parents are still unable to support them."

Burton, Lucinda:
37/529 - April 15, 1896.
"An inquest was this day held upon Lucinda
Burton, a lunatic, and recorded."

38/61 - November 5, 1896.
"It appearing to the satisfaction of the
Court that Lucinda Burton, a lunatic, was alive
in the 31st day of August 1896, and that she
had not sufficient estate for her support,
and that her husband was still unable to support
her, it is ordered that the allowance of $75.00
per annum for her support be continued from
the 15th day of April, 1896, the date of the
first inquest upon said lunatic, to the 31st
day of August 1896, the date of the second
inquest upon said lunatic, by virtue of which
said lunatic was sent to the asylum, and that
the same be copied and certified to the Auditor
for payment."

Burton, Sarah:
38/404 - November 11, 1898.
   "An inquest was this day held upon Sarah
Burton, an idiot and recorded."

39/41 - July 25, 1899.
   "It appearing to the satisfaction of the
Court from proof heard in open court that Sarah
Burton, an idiot, was alive on the 28th day
of December 1898, and had not estate sufficient
for her support, and that her parents were
still unable to support her, and that Sarah
Burton died on said 28th day of December 1898.
It is adjudged by the Court that said Sarah
Burton be allowed at the rate of $75.00 per
annum for her support from the date of the
inquest held upon her, viz: the 11th day of
November 1898, until and including the date
of her death, viz: the 28th day of December,
1898, which is ordered to be copied and certified to the Auditor of Public Accounts for
payment."

Carr, Amos:
37/7 August 23, 1892.
   "An inquest upon Amos Carr was this day held
and recorded."

39/500 - July 24, 1902.
   "Inquests were this day held upon Amos Carr,
Lavinia Flannigan and Isaiah Stepter and
recorded."

Carr, Malinda:
36/14 - August 29, 1888 (age 28).
   "This day the attorney filed an information
as follows: To Hon. A. E. Cole, Judge of the
Greenup Circuit Court: I am reliably informed
that Malinda Carr is a person of unsound mind
and an idiot, and therefore ask that a jury
be impaneled to pass upon the subject.
(signed) James H. Sallee, Commonwealth
Attorney, 14th Judicial District.
   Ordered by the court that Jerry Davidsen,
Esq., an attorney of this court be, and he
is hereby appointed to defend for and on behalf
of the person under trial.

To inquire comes a jury, towit: B. F. Young, Malcolm Jones, Henry Proffitt, Leander Martin, S. H. Glover, John C. Taylor, William May, Mordacai Walker, Francis Waring, N. W. Womack, Harvey McGinnis and Edward Holbrook, who being duly elected and sworn according to law, after hearing the evidence, returned the following verdict, viz: 'We, the jury, find from the evidence that Malinda Carr is a person of unsound mind and an idiot; that the cause of the unsoundness is not known and has existed from her birth; that she was born in Pennsylvania and resides in Greenup County, Kentucky, and is about 28 years old; that she was not brought into this State for the purpose of becoming a charge upon the Commonwealth, but was brought into the State when an infant and has since resided here; that she owns no estate of any kind, either in possession, reversion or remainder; that her father is dead and mother living and resides in Greenup County, Kentucky, and has not sufficient estate to support the person under trial, and said Malinda Carr is not capable of laboring in whole or in part for her support, and that she has not been heretofore adjudged an idiot.' (signed) Leander Martin, foreman.

It is therefore ordered that J. W. Womack be appointed a committee to take charge of said Malinda Carr and provide her with suitable diet, clothing, etc., and that he be allowed therefor at the rate of $75.00 per annum from this date, to be paid upon the further Order of this Court."

37/74 - April 4, 1893.

"It appearing to the satisfaction of the Court that Malinda Carr, an idiot, was alive and in the care of her committee up to the 24 day of December 1892, when she died, and had not sufficient estate for her support, and that her parents were unable to support her, it is ordered that the allowance of $75.00 per annum be continued from the last payment up to the 24 day of December 1892, and that the same be certified to the Auditor of Public Accounts.

It appearing to the satisfaction of the
Court that Malinda Carr, an idiot, died on
the 24th day of December 1892, and that J.
Watt Womack, her committee, necessarily expended
$10.00 for her burial expenses, it is ordered
that he be allowed the sum of $10.00 therefor,
and that the same be certified to the Auditor
for payment."

Carter, Anderson:
Z/150 - September 10, 1868.
"The Clerk of this court this day produced
the proceedings held under a Writ of Lunacy
in the case of Anderson Carter, a free man
of color, which are ordered to be filed, and
F. B. Trussell, the temporary committee of
said Anderson Carter, appointed by D. J. McCoy,
Judge of the Greenup County Court, before whom
said proceedings were had, this day produced
his statement which is filed and the same is
ordered to lie over until the 6th day of this
term for exceptions. It is ordered that said
Trussell be allowed $35.00 for his services
as temporary committee, to be retained by him
out of any money in his hands belonging to
said Anderson Carter."

Z/251 - December 3, 1868.
"F. B. Trussell, committee for Anderson
Carter, filed a final statement of his accounts
with the estate of said lunatic, which is
ordered to lie over for exceptions, and it
appearing that said Carter is restored to his
right mind, his committee is directed to pay
over to him any money that may remain in his
hands after the payment of the costs of the
proceedings had in his case and also return
to him any notes or evidences of debts, which
may be in his possession, belonging to said
Carter, and said committee is relieved from
further services as the committee of said
lunatic."

15/357 - August 16, 1872.
"It appearing to the satisfaction of the
court that Anderson Carter late of Greenup
County, deceased, has been dead more than three
months and that he died intestate, and no person

having applied for administration on the estate
of said decedent, it is ordered that the Sheriff
of this County take charge of the estate of
the said decedent and administer the same
according to law."

Caywood, Cordelia:
37/353 - April 3, 1895.
   "The proceedings of the Carter Circuit Court
in the case of Cordelia Caywood, an idiot,
was this day filed, and it appearing to the
satisfaction of the Court that said Cordelia
Caywood is still an idiot, and in the care
of her committee, and has not sufficient estate
for her support, and that her parents are still
unable to support her, it is ordered that the
allowance of $75.00 per annum for her support
be continued from the last payment, which is
ordered to be copied and certified to the
Auditor for payment.
   Ordered that Calvin Caywood be appointed
a committee to take charge of said Cordelia
Caywood and provide her with suitable diet,
clothing, etc. for her comfortable support.
He thereupon appeared in court and with John
Meyers as his surety, who is accepted and
approved by the Court, executed bond to the
Commonwealth of Kentucky, as committee aforesaid, conditioned according to law."

37/519 - April 10, 1896.
   "Calvin Caywood declining to further act
as committee for Cordelia Caywood, an idiot,
it is ordered that M. F. Caywood be appointed
committee for said idiot. He thereupon appeared
in Court and took the oath required by law
and executed bond with Calvin Caywood as his
security, conditioned according to law."

38/135 - April 14, 1897.
   "An inquest held in the Lewis Circuit Court
at its January term, 1897, upon Cordelia Caywood, an idiot, was this day filed, and it
appearing to the satisfaction of the Court
that said Cordelia Caywood is still alive and
that she has been removed to the County of
Greenup, and that she has not sufficient estate
for her support and that her parents are still

unable to support her, it is ordered that the
allowance of $75.00 for her support be continued
from the last payment. It further appearing
to the Court from proof heard in open Court
that M. F. Caywood, committee for said Cordelia
Caywood, has departed this life since his appoint
ment, it is ordered that Harvey Elkins be
appointed committee for said idiot. He thereupon appeared in Court and took the oath
required by law, and with William Darby as
his surety, who is approved and accepted by
the court, executed bond to the Commonwealth
of Kentucky, as committee aforesaid, conditioned
according to law."

38/158 - July 21, 1897.
    "W. F. Caywood filed a notice duly executed
and moved the Court to appoint him committee
for Cordelia Caywood, an idiot, in place of
Harvey Elkins, her present committee."

38/168 - July 22, 1897.
    "This cause being heard upon the Motion of
F. W. Caywood to be appointed committee for
Cordelia Caywood, an idiot, in place of Harvey
Elkins, and the Court being fully advised
adjudges that said motion be overruled, to
which said Caywood excepts."

38/224 - November 8, 1897.
    "It appearing to the satisfaction of the
Court that Cordelia Caywood, an idiot, was
alive on the 4th day of November, 1897, and
had not sufficient estate for her support,
and that her parents were still unable to
support her, and that said Cordelia Caywood
died on said 4th day of November, 1897, it
is ordered that the allowance of $75.00 per
annum for her support be continued from the
last payment until and including said 4th day
of November, 1897, and that the same be copied
and certified to the Auditor for payment."

Cluts (Clutts, Clutz), Mary Ann:
35/265 - February 8, 1887.
    "The proceedings before the Judge of the
Greenup County Court by which Mary Cluts was
adjudged a lunatic was this day produced and

filed, and it appearing to the satisfaction
of the Court that said Mary Cluts is a lunatic,
is still alive, and has not sufficient estate
for her support, and that her parents are still
unable to support her, it is ordered that A.
J. May be appointed a committee to take charge
of said Mary Cluts and provide her with suitable
diet, clothing, etc, and that he be allowed
therefor at the rate of $75.00 per annum to
be paid upon the further order of this Court.
The said May thereupon appeared in Court and
with William May as his security, who is
accepted and approved by the Court, executed
bond, conditioned according to law. And it
further appearing that said Mary Cluts is and
was a harmless lunatic, and that admittance
was refused in the Asylum, and that A. J. May
has kept and provided the said Mary Cluts with
suitable diet, clothing, etc. from the 25th
day of August 1885, the date of the inquest,
it is ordered that he be allowed at the rate
of $75.00 per annum therefor from the 25th
day of August 1885, and the same be copied
and certified to the Auditor of Public Accounts
for payment."

37/297 - November 7, 1894.
    "Ordered that Thomas May be and he is hereby
substituted as a committee for Mary Clutts,
a lunatic, in lieu of A. J. May. He thereupon
appeared in Court and took the oath required
by law and executed bond to the Commonwealth
of Kentucky, conditioned according to law,
with L. S. Tufts as his surety, who is approved
and accepted by the Court, and the same is
ordered to be certified to the Auditor."

39/372 - November 8, 1901.
    "It appearing to the satisfaction of the
court that Martha Jasper and Mary Clutts,
lunatics, and John Lawson, Christina McFarland,
William Vandergriff, Caroline Ham, Cora Horner,
Lavinia Flannigan, idiots, are still alive,
in the care of their committees and have not
estate sufficient for their support, and that
their parents are still unable to support them,
it is ordered that the allowance of $75.00
per annum each for their support be continued

from the last payment, and that the same be copied and certified to the Auditor of Public Accounts for payment."

Cooper, John J.:
V/364 - May 13, 1862 (age 22).
"On motion of the attorney for the Commonwealth, who represents that he has been informed that John Cooper of this county is a person of unsound mind, it is ordered that a writ of de idiota inquirendo issue, returnable immediately, to inquire into the state of mind of the said John Cooper and whether he hath any estate, and it is ordered that Edward Dulin, Esq., be appointed counsel for the said John Cooper. Whereupon the said John Cooper was brought into court and James Walker, Robert Johnson, William H. Warnock, J. L. Collins, James M. Craycraft, Jacob Willis, Francis Waring, A. Brysan, Benj. King, N. F. Thom, Jesse Davidson and Charles Callihan were impanelled, sworn and charged according to law as a jury of inquest under said writ, and having heard the evidence, returned the following verdict, towit: 'We, the jury, empanelled (sic) and sworn to inquire of the state of mind of John J. Cooper do say that he is in his 22nd year of age; that he is of unsound mind; that he has lost his mind since his birth, and since he was about 9 years of age; that it arose from fits, that his Father is dead, his Mother alive, but poor and no estate; that he has resided in Greenup County for about 18 years; was born in Lewis County, Kentucky and never lived anywhere except in Greenup and Lewis. That he has no estate of any kind, and is supported by the work of his Mother, an old Lady. That he is incapable of any labor, and we recommend him as a proper charge on the County.' (signed) Robt. Johnson, foreman.
Wherefore it is adjudged by the court that the said John Cooper is a person of unsound mind, and that he is a proper charge upon the County of Greenup, and it is ordered that the proceedings under said Writ and the Judgment of the court therein be certified to the County Court of said County."

W/236 - May 19, 1863 (age 22).
   "We, the jury, find that John Cooper is of
unsound mind; that he is a lunatic. He lost
his mind about 9 years of age, and being now
about 22 years of age. Don't know the cause
of loosing his mind; he was born in Greenup
County, Kentucky, and always has and still
resides there; he has no estate neither in
possession, reversion or remainder; his father
is dead, his mother is still living, with whom
he lives. She has no estate out of which to
support him, and he is incapable of doing any
labor for his own support. (signed)   S. B.
Hornbuckle, one of the jury.
   It is therefore adjudged that the said John
Cooper is a person of unsound mind; is a
lunatic; his Mother has no estate for his
support, and he is unable to labor for his
own support."

X/10 - November 10, 1863.
   "Ordered that Benjamin F. King be and he
is hereby appointed a committee for John Cooper,
who was found to be an idiot at the last term
of this Court. Whereupon he, together with
Wm. Corum as his surety, who is approved by
the Court, entered into a covenant as required
by law, and it appearing to the satisfaction
of the Court that the said John Cooper is still
alive, and an idiot, and has not sufficient
estate to support him, and that his parent
is still unable to support him, it is ordered
that $50.00 per annum be allowed for the support
of the said John Cooper, commencing in May
last, which is ordered to be certified to the
Auditor for payment."

X/478 - September 7, 1865 (age 27).
   "We, the jury, find that John Cooper, the
person under charge, is of unsound mind; that
is he lost his mind some 15 years age and is
an idiot by reason of fits. He was born in
Greenup County and is 27 years old and has
always lived in the state. He has no estate
of any kind. His Father is dead. His Mother
is alive, but has no estate. That he is not
capable of laboring in whole or in part for
his support, that he has been found to be a

person of unsound mind by a former inquest
in this Court. (signed) J. R. Barney, foreman.
    And the court being satisfied with the
inquest adjudges that said John Cooper is an
idiot, and has not sufficient estate for his
support, and his parents are unable to support
him, it is therefore ordered that the sum of
$50.00 per annum for his support and maintenance
from the last allowance payable to Benjamin
F. King, his committee."

Y/320 - March 7, 1867.
    "It appearing to the satisfaction of the
court that John J. Cooper, a lunatic, is still
alive and in the same condition he was at the
date of the last allowance made to him. It
is ordered by the court that the allowance
of $50.00 per annum be continued to said John
J. Cooper from time of his last allowance,
which is ordered to be copied and certified
to the Auditor."

26/6 - March 7, 1870.
    "It appearing to the satisfaction of the
Court that John Cooper, a pauper idiot of this
County, departed this life on the 27th day
of February last, it is ordered that the annual
allowance of $50.00 be continued to the com-
mittee of said John Cooper up to the date of
his death."

Culp, Frederick:
29/251 - March 19, 1874.
    "It appearing to the satisfaction of the
court that Frederick Culp, a pauper lunatic,
was confined in the Jail of Greenup County
in the custody and control of James P. Winter,
Jailer for Greenup County, as his committee,
and had not sufficient estate to support him,
and no friends or parents able to support him,
and that said pauper lunatic was taken care
of by said Jailer Winter from the 9th day of
August 1873, until the 10th day of September,
1873, making 33 days.
    It is therefore ordered that the allowance
at the rate of $200.00 per annum be paid said
Winters for the proportionable time he kept
said pauper lunatic, which amounts to the sum

of $18.08, and that the same be certified to
the Auditor for payment under the Act approved
March 28, 1872."

29/252 - March 19, 1874.
"It appearing to the satisfaction of the
court that Frederick Culp, a pauper lunatic,
was confined in the Greenup County Jail in
the custody and control of Charles Callihan,
Jailer for Greenup County, as his committee,
and had not sufficient estate for his support,
and no friends or parents able to support him,
and that said pauper lunatic was taken care
of by said Jailer Callihan from the 10th day
of June 1873 to the 9th day of August 1873,
making 61 days.
It is therefore ordered that the allowance
at the rate of $200.00 per annum be paid to
said Callihan for the proportionable time he
kept said pauper lunatic, which amounts to
the sum of $33.42, and that the same be certi-
fied to the Auditor for payment under the Act
approved March 28, 1872."

33/199 - March 26, 1880.
"Upon proof being made to the satisfaction
of the court that Frederick Culp, heretofore
found to be a lunatic, is still alive, in the
care of B. F. Warnock, his committee, and has
not sufficient estate for his support, and
that his parents are unable to support him,
it is ordered by the court that B. F. Warnock,
his committee, be allowed at the rate of $100.00
per annum for his support, which is ordered
to be copied and certified to the Auditor for
payment."

33/387 - March 17, 1881.
"Upon proof being made to the satisfaction
of the court that Fredrick Culp, heretofore
found to be a lunatic, is still alive, in the
care of his committee, and has not sufficient
estate for his support, and that his parents
are unable to support him, it is ordered by
the court that B. F. Warnock, his committee,
be allowed at the rate of $100.00 per annum
for his support from the last allowance, which
is ordered to be certified to the Auditor of
Public Accounts for payment."

34/31 - March 4, 1882 (age 53).
    "We, the jury, impaneled and sworn under
a writ from the Greenup Circuit Court directing
us to inquire if Frederick Culp of Greenup
County be of unsound mind, and having had a
view of said Frederick Culp in open court,
and having had evidence in relation to the
condition of his mind as well as estate, do
find that Frederick Culp is a lunatic, is about
53 years of age, and that he has no estate
of his own, and that he resides with his family,
who have not sufficient estate for one year's
maintenance of said Frederick Culp; that he
was born in Germany; that he was not destitute
of mind from infancy, cause of loss of mind
unknown; has heretofore been found a lunatic
by Judgment of this Court; sent to asylum and
returned as harmless; that he was not brought
into the state by any person for the purpose
of becoming a charge upon the Commonwealth,
and that he is incapable of laboring for his
own support. Given under our hands this 4th
day of March, 1882. (signed) James Bryan, foreman.
    It is therefore considered by the Court
that the said Frederick Culp is a lunatic,
that he is harmless; and that there be allowed
for his support at the rate of $100.00 per
annum payable to his committee; and that the
allowance be continued from the last payment,
which is ordered to be certified to the Auditor
for payment.
    Ordered that B. F. Warnock be appointed
a committee for said Frederick Culp, a lunatic.
He thereupon executed bond as required by law."

34/163 - September 6, 1883.
    It appearing to the satisfaction of the
Court that Frederick Culp, a lunatic, was still
alive and in the care of his committee up to
the 23rd day of June 1883, and had not sufficient estate for his support, and that his
parents were unable to support him, it is
ordered that the allowance of $75.00 per annum
be continued from the last payment and that
the same be certified to the auditor.
    It appearing to the satisfaction of the
Court that Frederick Culp, a lunatic, departed

this life on the 23rd day of June 1883, and
that his parents were unable to bury him, it
is ordered that B. F. Warnock, his committee
be allowed $10.00 for burial expenses and that
the same be certified to the auditor for
payment."

Damarin (Dameron, Damaron), Grant:
34/171 - August 25, 1884 (age 12).
    "Upon motion of the attorney for the Common-
wealth it is ordered that a writ of idiota
inquirendo issue in the case of Grant Damarin,
an idiot, ordered that George E. Roe, Esq.,
be appointed counsel for said Grant Damarin.
Thereupon came a jury, towit: F. B. Chinn,
Nathaniel Foster, G. E. Gammon, Willis Gholslen,
Willis Greenslate, Hugh Curry, Preston Burge,
Isaac Johnson, Luke Davissin, George Riffe,
John Rude, Thomas Montgomery. 'We, the jury,
impaneled and sworn to inquire into the condition of mind of Grant Damarin, and having had
a view of the said Grant Damarin in open Court,
and having heard the evidence in relation thereto, do find that the said Grant Damarin is
an idiot and the cause unknown, that he was
born in Ohio and is 12 years of age, that he
has resided in this County and State for two
years, that he has no estate in possession,
reversion or remainder, that his father is
dead, that his mother is living, that she has
no estate sufficient to support the said Grant
Damarin, that he was not brought into this
state for the purpose of becoming a charge
upon the Commonwealth, that he is not capable
of laboring in whole or in part for his
support.'"

34/198 - August 30, 1884.
    "It is ordered that B. F. Brown be appointed
committee to take charge of Grant Damrin and
provide him with suitable diet, clothing, etc.,
that he be allowed therefor at the rate of
$75.00 per annum from the finding of the jury,
to be paid upon the further order of this court.
Thereupon B. F. Brown appeared in court and
executed bond as committee aforesaid, which
is accepted and approved by the court and
ordered to be certified to the Auditor."

37/497 - April 8, 1896.
"It appearing to the satisfaction of the
Court that Grant Damarin, an idiot, was alive
in the 25th day of December 1895, and that
he had not sufficient estate for his support,
and that his parents were unable to support
him, it is ordered that the allowance of $75.00
per annum for his support be continued from
the last payment to the 25th day of December
1895, inclusive, that being the date of said
idiot's death, and that the same be certified
to the Auditor for payment."

Davidson, Mary:
U/585 - May 24, 1860 (age 22).
"Ordered that L. M. Cox be appointed attorney
for the Commonwealth, pro-tempore, and on his
motion, it is ordered that a writ of de lunatic
inquirendo issue, returnable immediately, to
inquire into the state of mind of Mary Davidson
and whether she has any estate, and it is
ordered that L. W. Andrews, a member of the
bar, is appointed to represent and protect
the interest and rights of said Mary Davidson.
Whereupon the said Mary Davidson was brought
into open court, and Alex Rankins, E. L.
Poynter, Wm. Brown, Lixuis Rife, James Osburn,
Hardin Riggs, O. F. McKoy, S. M. Rodgers, Jacob
Howe, O. N. Jones, Clem Swearingen, and Henry
Hayse were impanelled sworn and charged according to law as a jury of inquest over the said
writ and having heard the evidence returned
the following verdict, towit: 'We, the jury,
do find from the evidence that Mary Davidson,
the person whom we have in charge, is of unsound
mind and that she is a lunatic; that is, she
lost her mind since her birth and we are unable
to ascertain the cause of it; the first appear-
ance of it was manifested about 14 November
1859, and she seemed to be greatly excited
on the subject of religion at that time after
her insanity, and that was the way her insanity
first manifested itself; she was born in Greenup
County, Kentucky, in 1838, and has always
resided in this county and state. Resides
here and has not been brought into this state
by any person for the purpose of becoming a
charge upon it; she has no estate either in

possession, reversion or remainder; her parents
are alive and reside in this county, and has
not sufficient to support her, and she
is incapable of laboring in whole or in part
for her support. Her parents are quite old
and afflicted with bad health. The said Mary
Davidson is often violent and sometimes considered dangerous, and she is the constant
subject of care she may do some injury to
others.' (signed) O. F. McKoy.
    Whereupon it is adjudged by the court that
said Mary Davidson (is) a lunatic, and that
the date of the first attack was about the
14th day of November 1859, and that she be
taken to and confined in the lunatic asylum
at Lexington or Hopkinsville, and there to
remain until discharged therefrom, and that
the other facts found by the jury are true."

Davis, George:
35/381 - November 11, 1887.
    "It appearing to the satisfaction of the
court that Did Nicholls, Ben Beckworth, John
Murphy, Grant Damaron, Jacob Steenrod, John
Davis, George Davis, Vina Flanagan and George
Wurts, idiots, and Matt Hensley, a lunatic,
are still alive, in the care of their committees and have not sufficient estate for
their support, and that their parents are still
unable to support them, it is ordered that
the allowance of $75.00 per annum be continued
from the last payment, and that the same be
certified to the Auditor."

Davis, Hannah E.:
37/15 - August 24, 1892.
    "An inquest upon Hannah E. Davis was this
day held and the proceedings thereunder
recorded."

37/440 - November 6, 1895.
    "It appearing to the satisfaction of the
court that Hannah E. Davis and John Davis,
idiots, are still alive, in the care of their
committee, and have not sufficient estate for
their support, and that their parents are still
unable to support them, it is ordered that
the allowance of $75.00 each per annum be con-

tinued from the last payment and that the same
be certified to the Auditor for payment.
Ordered that Volney E. Thomson be appointed
a committee for said Hannah E. Davis and John
Davis in lieu of M. H. Merrill."

38/197 - November 3, 1897.
    "Ordered that Volney E. Thomson be removed
as committee for Hannah Davis, an idiot, and
that E. E. Fullerton be appointed committee
for said Hannah Davis in his place."

38/224 - November 8, 1897.
    "E. E. Fullerton, committee for Hannah Davis,
an idiot, appeared in court and took the oath
required by law and together with B. F. Bennett,
who is accepted and approved by the Court,
as his surety executed bond to the Commonwealth of Kentucky as committee aforesaid,
conditioned according to law."

39/368 - November 7, 1901.
    "It appearing to the satisfaction of the
court that Gracie Guilkey, Hannah Davis, Ella
Jennings, Birdie Traylor, William C. Kitts,
James A. Kitts, Bennie Adkins, John Murphy,
and Martha Wadkins, idiots, are still alive,
in the care of their committees, and have not
sufficient estate for their support, and that
their parents are still unable to support them,
it is ordered that the allowance of $75.00
per annum each for their support be continued
from the last payment, and that the same be
copied and certified to the Auditor of Public
Accounts for payment."

Davis, John:
35/85 - August 24, 1885 (age 20).
    "Upon motion of the attorney for the Common-
wealth, it is ordered that a writ of de idota
inquirendo issue in the case of John Davis,
an idiot, returnable immediately, to inquire
into the state of mind of said Davis, and it
is ordered that B. F. Bennett, Esq., be
appointed counsel for said Davis. Whereupon
came a jury towit: Thomas Traylor, John Pratt,
Mason G. Burns, Turner Crump, Fielding Harding,
W. F. Crump, Elias Leningten, John M. Stevensen,

Malcolm Jones, James F. Taylor, Newton Crisp
and H. H. Wampler, who being sworn according
to law returned the following verdict: 'We,
the jury, find from the evidence that John
Davis is a person of unsound mind and an idiot;
that the unsoundness of mind has existed from
birth; that he was born in Greenup County,
and resides in Greenup County and is 20 years
old; that he was not brought into this state
for the purpose of becoming a charge upon the
Commonwealth; that he owns no estate of any
kind; that his father is living and mother
and reside in Greenup County and they have
not estate sufficient to support the person
under trial, and said John Davis is not capable
of laboring in whole or in part for his
support.' (signed) James F. Taylor, foreman.
   It is ordered that S. H. Glover be appointed
committee to take charge of said John Davis
and provide him with suitable diet, clothing,
etc., and that he be allowed therefore at the
rate of $75.00 per annum from this date, to
be paid upon the further order of this Court.
Thereupon S. H. Glover appeared in Court and
with John B. Bush as his surety, who is accepted
and approved by the Court, executed bond as
committee aforesaid, conditioned according
to law, which is ordered to be certified to
the Auditor."

35/153 - February 23, 1886.
   "S. H. Glover, committee for John and Robert
Davis, idiots, filed his report, which is
examined and approved, and tendered his resignation as such committee, which is accepted.
Ordered that John H. Merrill be appointed committee for John Davis and Robert Davis, idiots.
He thereupon appeared in Court with S. H. Glover
as his surety, who is accepted and approved,
executed bond as committee aforesaid, conditioned according to law."

36/15 - August 29, 1888.
   "It appearing to the satisfaction of the
court that John Davis and Robert Davis, idiots,
are still in the care of their committee and
have not sufficient estate for their support,
and that their parents are still unable to

support them, it is ordered that the allowance
of $75.00 per annum each be continued from
the last payment and that the same be certified
to the Auditor.

Ordered that S. H. Glover be appointed committee for said John and Robert Davis to provide
them with suitable diet, clothing, etc. Whereupon he appeared in Court and with J. B. Mackoy
as his surety, who is accepted and approved
by the Court, executed bond to the Commonwealth
of Kentucky as committee aforesaid, conditioned
according to law."

36/231 - February 24, 1890.
"Ordered that B. F. King be appointed committee to take charge of John Davis and Robert
Davis and provide them with suitable diet,
clothing, etc. in place of Samuel H. Glover,
deceased. Whereupon he appeared in Court and
took the oath prescribed by law and with J.
E. Pollock as his security, who is accepted
and approved by the Court, executed bond to
the Commonwealth of Kentucky, conditioned
according to law."

37/440 - November 6, 1895.
"Ordered that Volney E. Thomson be appointed
a committee for said Hannah E. Davis and John
Davis in lieu of M. H. Merrill."

38/197 - November 3, 1897.
"Ordered that Volney E. Thomson be removed
as committee for John Davis, an idiot, and
that E. E. Fullerton be appointed committee
for said John Davis in his place."

38/224 - November 8, 1897.
"E. E. Fullerton, committee for John Davis,
an idiot, appeared in Court and took the oath
required by law, and together with B. F.
Bennett, who is accepted and approved by the
Court, as his surety executed bond to the
Commonwealth of Kentucky as committee aforesaid,
conditioned according to law."

38/487 - April 8, 1899.
"It appearing to the satisfaction of the
Court, from proof heard in open court, that

John Davis, an idiot, was alive on the 6th
day of November, 1898, and that he had not
sufficient estate for his support, and that
his parents were still unable to support him,
and that said John Davis died on said 6th day
of November, 1898, it is ordered that the
allowance of $75.00 per annum for the support
of said John Davis be continued from the last
payment until and including said 6th day of
November, 1898, and that the same be copied
and certified to the Auditor for payment."

Davis, Robert:
35/85 - August 24, 1885 (age 11).
  "Upon Motion of the attorney for the Commonwealth, it is ordered that a writ of deidota
inquirendo issue in the case of Robert Davis,
an idiot, returnable immediately, to inquire
into the state of mind of said Davis, and it
is ordered that B. F. Bennett, Esq., be
appointed counsel for said Davis. Whereupon
came a Jury, towit: Thomas Traylor, John Pratt,
Masson G. Burns, Turner Crump, F. Harding,
W. F. Crump, Elias Leningten, John M. Stevensen,
Malcolm Jones, James F. Taylor, Newton Crisp,
and H. H. Wampler, who being sworn according
to law returned the following verdict: 'We,
the jury, find from the evidence that Robert
Davis is a person of unsound mind and an idiot;
that the unsoundness of mind has existed from
birth; that he was born in Greenup County and
resides in Greenup County and is 11 years old;
that he was not brought into this state for
the purpose of becoming a charge upon the
Commonwealth; that he owns no estate of any
kind; that his father is living and mother,
and reside in Greenup County, and they have
not estate sufficient to support the person
under trial, and said Robert Davis is not
capable of laboring in whole or in part for
his support.' (signed) James F. Taylor, foreman.
  It is therefore ordered that S. H. Glover
be appointed a committee to take charge of
Robert Davis and provide him with suitable
diet, clothing etc., and that he be allowed
therefor at the rate of $75.00 per annum from
this date, to be paid upon the further order
of this Court.

The said S. H. Glover, committee of Robert
Davis, appeared in Court and with John B. Bush
as his surety, who is accepted and approved
by the Court, executed bond as committee aforesaid, conditioned according to law."

35/153 - February 23, 1886.
"S. H. Glover, committee for John and Robert
Davis, idiots, filed his report which is
examined and approved and tendered his resignation as such committee, which is accepted.
Ordered that John H. Merrill be appointed committee for John Davis and Robert Davis, idiots.
He thereupon appeared in Court with S. H. Glover
as his surety, who is accepted and approved,
executed bond as committee aforesaid, conditioned according to law."

36/15 - August 29, 1888.
"It appearing to the satisfaction of the
court that John Davis and Robert Davis, idiots,
are still in the care of their committee and
have not sufficient estate for their support,
and that their parents are still unable to
support them, it is ordered that the allowance
of $75.00 per annum each be continued from
the last payment and that the same be certified
to the Auditor.
Ordered that S. H. Glover be appointed committee for said John and Robert Davis to provide
them with suitable diet, clothing, etc. Whereupon he appeared in Court and with J. B. Mackoy
as his surety, who is accepted and approved
by the Court, executed bond to the Commonwealth
of Kentucky as committee aforesaid, conditioned
according to law."

36/231 - February 24, 1890.
"Ordered that B. F. King be appointed committee to take charge of John Davis and Robert
Davis and provide them with suitable diet,
clothing, etc., in place of Samuel H. Glover,
deceased. Whereupon he appeared in Court and
took the oath prescribed by law and with J.
E. Pollock as his security, who is accepted
and approved by the Court, executed bond to
the Commonwealth of Kentucky, conditioned
according to law."

36/425 - August 25, 1891.
"It appearing to the satisfaction of the
court that Robert Davis, an idiot, was alive
up to the 9th day of May 1891, and in the care
of his committee, and had not sufficient estate
for his support, and that his parents were
unable to support him, it is ordered that the
allowance of $75.00 per annum be continued
from the last payment up to the 9th day of
May, 1891, when the said Davis died, and that
the same be certified to the Auditor of Public
Accounts."

"It appearing to the satisfaction of the court
that B. F. King, committee for Robert Davis,
an idiot, who died in the 9th day of May, 1891,
expended $3.00 for the burial of said idiot,
it is ordered that he be allowed $3.00, the
amount expended as aforesaid, and that the
same be copied and certified to the Auditor
for payment."

Day, Rebecca J.:
37/268 - July 18, 1894.
"A transcript of the proceedings had in the
Morgan Circuit Court in the case of Rebecca
J. Day, an idiot, was this day produced and
filed, and it is ordered that W. M. Stevens
be and he is hereby appointed a committee to
take charge of said idiot and provide her with
suitable diet, clothing, etc. He thereupon
appeared in Court and with James E. Morton
as his surety, who is accepted and approved
by the court, executed bond to the Commonwealth
of Kentucky as committee aforesaid, conditioned
according to law. It appearing to the satisfaction of the Court that said Rebecca J. Day,
an idiot, is still alive in the care of her
committee, and has not sufficient estate for
her support and that her parents are still
unable to support her, it is ordered that the
allowance of $75.00 per annum for her support
be continued from the last payment and that
the same be copied and certified to the Auditor
of Public Accounts."

37/491 - April 7, 1896.

"It appearing to the satisfaction of the
court that Jennie Belle Smith and Martha Jasper,
lunatics, and Rebecca J. Day, Birdie Traylor,
Gracie Guilkey and William C. Kitts, idiots,
are still alive, in the care of their committees, and have not sufficient estate for
their support, and that their parents are still
unable to support them, it is ordered that
the allowance of $75.00 each per annum for
their support be continued from the last payment, and that the same be certified to the
Auditor for payment."

Duncan, William M.:
39/86 November 13, 1899.
"It appearing to the satisfaction of the
court that W. M. Duncan, a lunatic, and
Christina McFarland, Cora Horner, and Caroline
Ham, idiots, are still alive, in the care of
their committees, and have not sufficient estate
for their support, and that their parents are
still unable to support them, it is ordered
that the allowance of $75.00 per annum each
for their support be continued from the last
payment and that the same be copied and certified to the Auditor of Public Accounts for
payment."

39/372 - November 8, 1901.
"It appearing to the satisfaction of the
Court that William Duncan, a lunatic, was alive
on the 16th day of June, 1901, and had not
estate sufficient for his support, and that
his parents are still unable to support him,
and that said William Duncan left Greenup County
on said 16th day of June, 1901, it is ordered
that the allowance of $75.00 per annum for
his support be continued from the last payment
until and including said 16th day of June,
1901, it is ordered to be copied and certified
to the Auditor of Public Accounts for payment."

Ferguson, Sreany:
39/232 - November 8, 1900.
"It appearing to the satisfaction of the
court that Martha Jasper, a lunatic, and Sreany
Ferguson, James A. Kitts, William C. Kitts,
John Murphy, Bennie Adkins, Bertha Traylor,

Thomas Hill, Martha Wadkins, Christina McFarland
and Hannah Davis, idiots, and Mary Clutts,
a lunatic, are still alive, in the care of
their committees and have not sufficient estate
for their support, and that their parents are
still unable to support them, it is ordered
that the allowance of $75.00 per annum each
for their support be continued from the last
payment, and that the same be copied and certified to the Auditor of Public Accounts for
payment."

39/71- November 9, 1899.
"An inquest was this day held upon Sreany
Ferguson, a Harmless Imbecile, and recorded."

Fiffe, Marvilla:
33/398 - August 22, 1881 (age 12).
"Upon motion of the attorney for the Commonwealth, it is ordered that a writ de idiota
inquirendo issue in the case of Marvilla Fiffe,
an idiot, returnable immediately, to inquire
into the state of mind of said Marvilla Fiffe,
and it is ordered that George E. Roe, Esquire,
be appointed counsel for said Marvilla Fiffe.
Whereupon came a jury, towit: Samuel S. Hill,
J. L. Bryson, Francis Waring, Nathaniel Foster,
Henry Mead, Jr., H. M. Rye, Thomas Jones, James
Gholsten, Elias Ware, David L. Downs, M. A.
Warnock, and Jacob Willis, who being sworn
according to law returned the following verdict:
'We, the Jury, impaneled and sworn under a
Writ from the Greenup Circuit Court directing
us to inquire if Marville Fiffe of Greenup
County be of unsound mind, and having had a
view of said Marvilla Fiffe in open Court,
and having had evidence in relation to the
condition of her mind as well as estate, do
find that Marvilla Fiffe is an idiot, is about
12 years of age, and that she has no estate
of her own; that she resides with her parents
who have not sufficient estate for one year's
maintenance of said Marvilla Fiffe; that she
was born in Morgan County, Kentucky; that she
was destitute of mind from infancy, and that
she was not brought into the state by any person
for the purpose of becoming a charge upon the
Commonwealth, and that she is incapable of

laboring for her own support.' Given under
our hands and seal this 22nd day of August
1881. (signed)   Jacob Willis, foreman."

34/3 - February 27, 1882.
    "Upon proof being made to the satisfaction
of the court that Marvilla Fiffe, heretofore
found to be an idiot, is still alive, in the
care of Lewis Nicholls, her committee, and
has not sufficient estate for her support,
and that her parents are still unable to support
her, it is ordered by the court that Lewis
Nicholls, her committee, be allowed at the
rate of $75.00 per annum for her support from
the last allowance, which is ordered to be
certified to the Auditor for payment."

34/57 - August 31, 1882.
    "Upon proof being made to the satisfaction
of the Court that Marvella Fiffe, heretofore
found to be an idiot, was alive in the care
of Lewis Nicholls, her committe, up to the
1st day of June 1882, and had not sufficient
estate for her support, and that her parents
were unable to support her, it is ordered by
the Court that Lewis Nicholls her committee
be allowed at the rate of $75.00 per annum
for her support from the last allowance, which
is ordered to be copied and certified to the
Auditor of Public Accounts for payment."

Flannagan (Flannigan, Flannagen, Flanigan),
Lavenia (Lavinia, Vina):
35/164 - February 24, 1886 (age 11).
    "Upon motion of the attorney for the Common-
wealth, it is ordered that a writ de idota
inquirendo issue in the case of Lavenia
Flannagan, an idiot, returnable immediately,
to inquire into the state of mind of said
Flannagan, and it is ordered that D. J. McCoy
be appointed counsel for said Flannagan. Whereupon came a jury towit: Jasper Rake, L. P.
Harrison, O. S. Riffe, D. S. Mitchell, R. F.
Dingess, G. W. Robinson, William Bradley, John
Patton, John Riggs, Arch Conway, James Burkley,
and E. P. Davenport, who being sworn according
to law returned the following verdict: 'We,
the jury, find from the evidence that Lavenia

Flannagan is a person of unsound mind and an
idiot; that the unsoundness of mind has existed
from birth; that she was born in Greenup County,
Kentucky, and resides in Greenup County,
Kentucky, and is 11 years old; that she was
not brought into this state for the purpose
of becoming a charge upon the Commonwealth;
that she owns no estate of any kind; that her
father is dead and mother is living and resides
in Greenup County, Kentucky, and she has not
estate sufficient to support the person under
trial, and said Lavenia Flannagan is not capable
of laboring in whole or in part for her
support.' (signed) E. P. Davenport, Foreman.
        It is therefore ordered that J. H. Merrill
be appointed a committee to take charge of
said Lavenia Flannagan and provide her with
suitable diet, clothing, etc., and that he
be allowed therefor at the rate of $75.00 per
annum from this date, to be paid upon the further orders of this court."

35/281 - March 2, 1887.
        "It appearing to the satisfaction of the
court that Lavenia Flannagan, an idiot, is
still alive, in the care of her committee,
and has not sufficient estate for her support,
and that her parents are still unable to support her, it is ordered that the allowance
of $75.00 per annum for her support be paid
her committee from the finding of the jury
at a former term of this court, and that the
same be certified to the Auditor of Public
Accounts.
        John Merrill, committee for Lavenia
Flannagan, appeared in Court and with B. F.
Bennett as his security, who is accepted and
approved by the court, executed a bond as committee aforesaid, conditioned according to
law."

37/62 - September 10, 1892.
        "It appearing to the satisfaction of the
court that Lavinia Flannagan, an idiot, is
still alive and in the care of Mary H. Merrill,
her committee, and has not sufficient estate
for her support, and that her parents are still
unable to support her, it is ordered that the

allowance of $75.00 per annum be continued
from the finding of the jury at a former term
and that the same be certified to the Auditor
of Public Accounts."

37/463 - November 11, 1895.
    "M. H. Merrill declining to further act as
committee for Lavenia Flannigan, an idiot,
it is ordered that John T. McNeal be appointed
committee for said Lavena Flannigan."

39/500 - July 24, 1902.
    "Inquests were this day held upon Amos Carr,
Lavinia Flannigan, and Isaiah Stepter and
recorded.

Foster, Elizabeth:
N/333 - April 8, 1843 (age 16).
    "On Motion of the Attorney for the Common-
wealth, it is ordered that the Sheriff of
Greenup County summon twelve housekeepers of
this county to appear here immediately to
inquire whether Elizabeth Foster, who is now
in open court, be or be not of sound mind,
and if she be of unsound mind, whether she
was so from the time of her birth, or became
so afterwards, and what property she has, and
thereupon came a jury, to-wit: John C. Kouns,
Allen Myers, Jesse Davidson, Thomas I. Garrett,
Samuel Seaton, John Culver, A. A. Clutz,
Harrison Hunt, Charles Kingsbury, David Poynter,
Alexander Patton and N. F. Thom, who being
elected, tried and sworn well and truly to
inquire into and ascertain the facts of which
they were summoned to inquire, upon their oaths
do say that the said Elizabeth Foster is an
idiot and was at the time of her birth; that
she is now 16 years of age; that she is living
with her father who is in very indigent circumstances with a large family, and that she hath
no estate whatsoever. The said Elizabeth Foster
was in open court, witnesses were examined,
and counsel appeared.
    It is therefore ordered that it be certified
to the Auditor of Public Accounts that John
B. Foster, who is appointed a committee to
take care of the said Elizabeth Foster, is
entitled at the rate of $50.00 per annum from

this date for the use and support of the said
Elizabeth Foster."

O/305 - October 27, 1846 (age 20).
   "We, the jury, having had a view of said
Elizabeth Foster and having heard evidence
in relation to the condition of her mind as
well as estate, do find said Elizabeth Foster
is an idiot, is about 20 years of age and has
no estate of her own; that she resides with
her parents, who have not sufficient estate
for a years maintenance of said Elizabeth
Foster. That said Elizabeth is incapable of
any labor for her support and that she was
born in the County of Greenup and State of
Kentucky. It is ordered that it be certified
to the Auditor of Public Accounts that John
B. Foster, the committee for said Elizabeth
Foster, is entitled to receive at the rate
of $50.00 per annum from the 27th day of April,
1846, to this date, 29 October 1846, for the
use, support and maintenance of said Elizabeth
Foster."

R/305- May 30, 1855 (age 29).
   "We, the jury, find that Elizabeth Foster
has been an idiot from her birth; that she
is about 29 years old; that she was born in
Greenup County and been here ever since; that
she is single and never spoke a word in her
life, has no relatives who are insane, don't
know any cause of idiotcy, no attempt at
suicide, continual state of frenzy and no lucid
intervals. She has to be constantly attended
by some one, no injury about her head or bodily
diseases or sores; that she has been found
an idiot by the verdict of a jury and judgment
of this court; that no change has taken place
in her mind, and that no estate has come or
descended to her since that time; that her
father and mother are still living and unable
to support her and that she has no estate out
of which to support her.
   It is therefore ordered that John B. Foster,
her father, be appointed a committee to take
charge of said Elizabeth Foster and provide
her with suitable diet, clothing, etc., and
that he be allowed therefor at the rate of

$50.00 per annum from the last allowance to
her, which is ordered to be certified to the
Auditor of Public Accounts for payment."

V/259 - November 28, 1860 (age 34).
   "We, the jury, find that Elizabeth Foster
is an idiot, she was born in this County and
resides here and is about 34 years old and
was not brought from any other state for the
purpose of becoming a charge upon the Commonwealth. She has always resided here except
about two years in Ohio. She has no estate
in possession, reversion or remainder, her
Father is dead--her Mother is alive, but has
not estate sufficient to support her, her Mother
resides in this County, that said idiot is
incapable of laboring at all for her support.
She has heretofore been found an idiot by the
verdict of a jury and Judgment of this court,
no change has since then taken place in her
mind, physical condition or estate. (signed)
Cyrus VanBibber, foreman.
   Wherefore it is adjudged by the court that
the said Elizabeth Foster is an idiot and has
not estate for her support, and her parents
are unable to support her. Wherefore it is
adjudged by the court that the sum of $50.00
per annum be allowed to Harrison G. Foster,
the committee of said Elizabeth Foster, for
her support and maintenance from the last allowance for her."

W/186 - May 12, 1863.
   "It appearing to the satisfaction of the
Court that Harrison Foster, the former committee
of Elizabeth Foster, has departed this life,
it is ordered that Lafayette Foster be appointed
in the room and stead of the said Harrison
Foster.
   And it appearing to the satisfaction of
the Court that said Elizabeth Foster, an idiot,
is still alive, in the care of her committee,
and has not sufficient estate for her support,
and that her parents are still unable to support
her, it is ordered that the allowance of $50.00
per annum be continued from the last payment,
and that the same be certified to the Auditor."

X/457 - September 5, 1865 (age 38).
"Upon the motion of attorney for the Common-
wealth, it is ordered that a Writ of De iodta
inquirendo issue in the case of Elizabeth
Foster, and it is ordered that George E. Roe,
Esq., be appointed as counsel for said Elizabeth
Foster. Which said Elizabeth Foster being
personally in open court. Whereupon came a
jury, towit: Charles R. Callihan, John L.
Collins, Marshall Clark, John P. B. Hill, James
T. Warnock, Ed S. Poynter, James Downs, John
R. Barney, Lewis Nicholls, James Osborn, Charles
Callihan and John H. Sennett, who being sworn
according to law returned the following verdict,
towit: 'We, the jury, find that Elizabeth
Foster, the person under charge, is an idiot;
that is she has been destitute of mind from
infancy, she was born in Greenup County,
Kentucky, and is 38 years old and has not been
brought into the state for the purpose of becoming a charge upon the state. Her father was
dead, her mother is alive. She has no estate.
She is not capable of laboring in whole or
in part for her support. She was found to
be an idiot by a former inquest in this court.'
(signed) Lewis Nicholls.
    And the court being satisfied with the
inquest adjudges that the said Elizabeth Foster
is an idiot and has not any estate for her
support and her parents are unable to support
her. It is therefore ordered that the sum
of $50.00 per annum be allowed for her support
and maintenance from the last allowance, payable
to Lafayette Foster, her committee."

26/177 - September 12, 1870 (age 40).
"We, the jury, find that Elizabeth Foster,
whose presence in Court has been dispensed
with, owing to her condition, in pursuance
to the certificate of the two physicians filed,
and we find her of unsound mind and that she
is an idiot, being destitute of mind ever since
her birth, she was born in the State and is
about 40 years of age, she has no estate of
any kind for her support. Her father is dead
and she lives with her mother, who lives in
Greenup County and that her mother has not
estate sufficient for her support, and that

she is not capable in whole or part to labor
for her support. We further find that she
has heretofore been found to be an idiot by
the verdict and judgment of this Court, and
that no change for the better has taken place
in her condition or estate since the original
inquest. (signed) F. Bennett, foreman
And it is further ordered that Lafayette
Foster be continued as committee to take charge
of said Elizabeth Foster and provide her with
suitable diet, clothing, etc., and that the
allowance of $50.00 per annum be continued
from the last allowance, which is ordered to
be certified to the Auditor."

31/77 - September 11, 1875.
"Upon motion of the attorney for the Common-
wealth, it is ordered that a writ of de idiota
inquirendo issue in the case of Elizabeth
Foster, an idiot, returnable immediately, to
inquire into the state of mind of said
Elizabeth; and it is ordered that Thomas H.
Paynter be appointed counsel for said Elizabeth.
Whereupon came a jury, towit: David Artist,
John Bush, Elias Oliver, Nathaniel Foster,
Alexander Patton, Miles Tumbleson, Samuel Hill,
Robert Stewart, Samuel Critzer, Andrew Simmends,
Thomas Wilson, Lewis Gray, who being sworn
according to law, returned the following
verdict, towit: 'We, the jury, find that the
person under trial, Elizabeth Foster, is of
unsound mind and a lunatic; that she was born
in Greenup County, Kentucky, about 1830, and
has always resided in said County; that she
has no estate in possession, reversion or
remainder; that her father is dead, but her
mother is alive and resides in said County
but she has no estate of any kind; that said
Elizabeth Foster is not capable of laboring
to any extent for her support. We find further
that the father of said Elizabeth died in said
County about 1854, leaving about 180 acres
of land, 100 acres of hill and 80 acres of
botton land in Greenup County, Kentucky, and
some stock and personal property and by Will
devised all of said real and personal estate
to Lafayette Foster and H. G. Foster, upon
condition that they, said Foster, should pay

the debts of said decedent, keep the family
of said decedent including said idiot,
Elizabeth Foster. Said H. G. Foster is now
dead; that said land is worth $25.00 in rental
values per year after paying for keeping up
all necessary repairs, paying taxes $125; that
the interest of said Elizabeth Foster in said
rental would be $25.00.' (signed) Samuel L.
Hill, Foreman.

And it is therefore ordered that Lafayette
Foster, be appointed a committee to take charge
of said Elizabeth Foster and provide her with
suitable diet, clothing, etc. and that he be
allowed therefor at the rate of $50.00 per
annum from this date. It is further ordered
that said Elizabeth Foster's committee be
required to give bond and security for the
faithful performance of his duty in this case;
and the said Lafayette Foster gave bond with
Miles Tumblesen security, according to this
order, and the same was accepted by the Court,
and ordered to be certified to the Auditor."

31/295 - March 17, 1876.
"It appearing to the satisfaction of the
court that Elizabeth Foster, an idiot, is still
alive and in the charge of her committee, and
that she has not sufficient estate for her
support and that her parents are unable to
support her, it is ordered that the allowance
of $50.00 per annum be continued from the last
payment, which is ordered to be certified to
the Auditor."

Freoter Gottfried:
S/202 - November 13, 1856.
"On motion of the attorney for the Commonwealth, it is ordered that a writ of de lunatico
inquirendo issue against Gottfried Freoter,
who is suppose to be a lunatic, returnable
immediately, to inquire into the state of mind
of said Gottfried Freoter, and it is ordered
that L. W. Andrews, Esq., be appointed counsel
for said Gottfried Freoter. Whereupon the
said Gottfried Freoter was brought into court,
and thereupon came a jury, towit: I. N. Bates,
foreman, Moses Mackoy, Joseph B. Puthuff, David
D. Geiger, William Williams, John Russell,

George S. Poage, Thomas Crum, R. M. Biggs,
Benjamin F. Lawson, Jonathan Horn, and Nicholas
Savage who being duly sworn according to law,
upon their oaths returned the following verdict,
towit: 'We, the Jury, find that Gottfried
Freoter is unsound in mind and a lunatic; that
he has lost his mind from his birth, the cause
of which Jury are not able to ascertain; that
his birth place is Baden in Germany; that he
was not brought into this state for the purpose
of becoming a charge upon this Commonwealth;
that he has $7.60 in money and $40.00 reported
due to him from a Mr. Huffman at the Pennsylvania Furnace; that we are not able to ascertain
whether his parents are alive nor whether they
have estate sufficient to support him, and
he is only in part able to labor for his
support.' (signed)   J. N. Bates, Moses Mackoy,
Joseph Puthuff, David D. Geiger, William
Williams, John Russell, George S. Poage, Thomas
Crum, R. M. Biggs, Benj. F. Lawson, Jonathan
Horn, Nicholas Savage
     It is therefore adjudged by the court that
the said Gottfried Freoter is a lunatic."

Friley, William:
38/213 - November 6, 1897.
     "It appearing to the satisfaction of the
Court that George Wurts, Amos Carr, Celia
Leathers, Lucy Middaugh, Minnie McGinnis, Did
Nicholls, Isaiah Stepter, John Traylor, Minta
Traylor, William Friley, and Mary Griffith,
idiots, and John Wood and Mary Wheeler,
lunatics, are still alive, in the care of their
committees and have not sufficient estate for
their support, and that their parents are still
unable to support them, it is ordered that
the allowance of $75.00 each per annum for
their support be continued from the last payment, and that the same be copied and certified
to the Auditor for payment."

39/71 - November 9, 1899.
     "It appearing to the satisfaction of the
court that Mary Clutts, Mary Wheeler, Jennie
Belle Smith, and John Wood, lunatics, and Ella
Jennings, Bennie Adkins, John Murphy, Martha
Wadkins, William C. Kitts, James A. Kitts,

Bertha Traylor, George Wurts, Cynthia Ann
Burton, Amos Carr, William Friley, Mary
Griffith, Celia Leathers, Minnie McGinnis,
Lucy Middaugh, Did Nicholls, John Traylor,
Mintie Traylor, Isaiah Stepter, and Hannah
Davis, idiots, are still alive, in the care
of their committees, and have not estate sufficient for their support, and that their parents
are still unable to support them, it is ordered
that the allowance of $75.00 per annum each
for their support be continued from the last
payment, and that the same be copied and certified to the Auditor of Public Accounts for
payment."

Gantz, Sarah:
33/182 - August 24, 1880.
    "Upon proof being made to the satisfaction
of the court that Sarah Gantz, heretofore found
to be an idiot, is still alive and in the care
of Sidney Gantz, her committee, and has not
sufficient estate for her support, and that
her parents are still unable to support her,
it is ordered by the court that Sidney Gantz,
her committee, be allowed at the rate of $50.00
per annum from the last allowance, which is
ordered to be certified to the Auditor of Public
Accounts for payment."

34/55 - August 31, 1882 (age 20).
    "We, the jury, impaneled and sworn under
a writ from the Greenup Circuit Court directing
us to inquire if Sarah Gantz of Greenup be
of unsound mind, and having had a view of said
Sarah Gantz in open court, and having had
evidence in relation to the condition of her
mind as well as estate, do find that said Sarah
Gantz is an idiot, is about 20 years of age,
and that she has a small piece of land, but
not sufficient to yield her any support, if
rented out would bring about $15.00 per year;
that she resides with her mother who has not
sufficient estate for one year's maintenance
of said Sarah Gantz; that her father is dead,
that she was born in Greenup County; that she
was destitute of mind from infancy, and that
she was not brought into the state by any
person for the purpose of becoming a charge

upon the Commonwealth, and that she is (not)
capable of laboring for her own support, and
that she has heretofore been found an idiot.
(signed) T. J. Thompson.

It is therefore considered that the said
Sarah Gantz is an idiot, and that there be
allowed to clothe, support and maintain her
the sum of $75.00 per annum."

34/121 - August 27, 1883.

"It appearing to the satisfaction of the
Court that Sarah Gantz, an idiot, was alive
up to the 24th day of July 1883 and in the
care of her committee and had not sufficient
estate for her support, and that her parents
were unable to support her, it is ordered that
the allowance of $75.00 per annum be continued
from the last payment up to the 24 day of July,
1883, and that the same be certified to the
auditor.

It appearing to the satisfaction of the
Court that Sarah Gantz, an idiot, died on the
24 day of July, 1883, it is ordered that her
committee be allowed $10.00 for her burial
expenses, which is ordered to be certified
to the auditor for payment."

Geno (Ganoe), Magdalene (Magdalin):
35/218 - August 24, 1886 (age 13).

"Upon motion of the attorney for the Commonwealth, it is ordered that a writ of de idiota
inquirendo issue in the case of Magdalin Geno,
ordered that Thomas H. Paynter, Esq., be
appointed counsel for the said Magdalin Geno.
Thereupon came a jury, towit: George W. Walker,
F. C. Robb, George W. Thompson, James Halmes,
Edward Callihan, Henderson Wampler, John McNeal,
E. N. Winn, Jacob Rake, Thomas Wilson, John
Taylor and M. F. Tumblesen, who were duly sworn
and having heard the evidence returned the
following verdict: 'We, the jury, impaneled
and sworn to ascertain whether or not Magadlin
Geno is a person of unsound mind, and having
had a view of the said Magadlin Geno in open
court, and having heard the evidence in relation
thereto, do find that the said Magadlin Geno
is a person of unsound mind and a lunatic,
cause unknown; that she was born in the State

of Virginia and is 13 years of age, and has
resided in this County and State for 8 years;
that she has no estate in possession, reversion
or remainder; that her father is living, mother
dead; that they have no estate sufficient to
support the person under trial; that she is
incapable of laboring in whole or in part for
her own support and was not brought into this
County or State for the purpose of becoming
a charge upon the Commonwealth.' This 24 August
1886. (signed) F. C. Robb, foreman.
    It is therefore ordered that James Hoop
be appointed a committee to take charge of
said Magadalin Geno and provide her with sufficient diet, clothing etc. The said James Hoop
appeared in court and took the oath required
by law and with Alvin B. Mortin as his security,
who is accepted and approved by the court,
executed a covenant to the Commonwealth of
Kentucky as committee aforesaid, conditioned
according to law."

36/91 - February 26, 1889.
    "It appearing to the satisfaction of the
Court that Magdalena Ganoe, an idiot, was alive
and in the care of her committee up to the
31st day of December 1888, and had not sufficient estate for her support, and that her
parents were unable to support her, it is
ordered that the allowance of $75.00 per annum
for her support be continued from the last
payment up to the 31st day of December 1888,
the date of her death, and it further appearing
that the committee had necessarily expended
$10.00 for the burial of said Magdalena Ganoe,
it is ordered that he be allowed the sum of
$10.00 for burial expenses, and that the same
be certified to the Auditor of Public Accounts."

Gilkerson, James:
0/346 - April 26, 1847 (age 70).
    "On motion of the attorney for the Common-
wealth, who represents that James Gilkerson
of this county is a person of unsound mind,
it is ordered that a Writ de lunatico inquireno
issue for the purpose of inquiring into the
state of the mind of said James Gilkerson,
and whether he has any estate, and if any,

the nature and extent thereof, and thereupon
a jury was summonded, towit: Walter Smiley,
Joshua Glover, Deupolle Valodine, Thomas Kay,
John Montgomery, Hugh Jackson, Charles Stewart,
William Anderson, Charles Craycraft, Seymore
Hardin, Henry Puthuff, and William Craycraft,
who were sworn and charged to inquire, and
having heard the evidence returned to following
veridict, towit, viz: 'We, the jury, find
that said James Gilkerson is a person of unsound
mind; that he is about 70 years of age; by
occupation a farmer; is a married man; has
been insane about five years; his disposition
is not materially changed; that he has never
attempted to commit suicide; that he is not
subject to fits; that his education is limited;
that he has no insane relations; that he is
kind and generous to his relations, and that
his general health is good, and that he is
a person of unsound mind and has been so for
five years past, and that it is the first and
only attack.'"

O/351 - April 27, 1847.
    "Ordered that James Rouse be appointed a
Committee to take charge of James Gilkerson,
a lunatic. Whereupon he, together with William
Hampton and William S. Geiger as his securities,
came into Court and executed and acknowledged
bond in the penalty of $1,000.00, conditioned
according to law."

Glassford, Sally:
Eo/371 - April 24, 1820.
    "Ordered that a writ of deidaoto issue
directed to the Sheriff of this County commanding him to impannell a legal Jury to inquire
into the sanity of Sally Glassford, returnable
to the second day of this term. (No entry
was found on 2nd day of term)

G/355 - October 1, 1827 (age 19).
    "On motion of James Ruggles, Sr., a Jury
was sworn to inquire into the state of mind
of Sally Glassford who is now living with him,
towit: Thomas Fairman, John Patton, Squire
Barney, John N. Howe, Amos Richardson, James
Osburn, David Morton, James Week, John Poage,

Martin Culp, John Bush, and Charles Craycraft,
who returned the following verdict, towit:
'We, the jury, impanelled and sworn to inquire
into the state of mind of Sally Glassford find
that she is, and has been from her birth, an
idiot, that she is about 19 years of age, and
it is ordered that James Ruggles, Sr., be
appointed a committee to keep and maintain
said Sally Glassford and that he be allowed
for keeping said Sally Glassford from the 15th
day of February last at the rate of $50.00
per annum, which is ordered to be certified
to the Auditor of Public Accounts.'"

H/235 - April 8, 1830.
    "Ordered that Elzy Virgin be appointed a
committee to keep and maintain Sally Glassford
who was found to be an idiot at a former term
of this court, in the room and stead of James
Ruggles, who has removed out of this state,
and it appearing to the satisfaction of the
court that said Sally Glassford still lives
and continues in the same situation, it is
therefore ordered to be certified to the Auditor
of Public Accounts that the said Elzy Virgin
is entitled at the rate of $50.00 per annum
from the 9th day of October, 1829 up to this
time for the use and support of said Sally
Glassford, one-half of which is to be paid
to William Jordan, Jr., with whom the said
Sally Glassford resided three months, the
residue is to be paid to James Ruggles the
former committee."

H/268 - July 5, 1830.
    "Ordered that Andrew Zornes be appointed
a committee to keep and maintain Sally Glassford, who was found to be an idiot at a former
term of this court, in the room and stead of
Elzy Virgin, and it appearing to the satisfaction of the court that said Sally Glassford
still lives and continues in the same situation,
it is therefore ordered to be certified to
the Auditor of Public Accounts that said Andrew
Zornes is entitled at the rate of $50.00 per
annum from the 8th day of April, 1830 up to
this date for the use and support of said Sally
Glassford."

L/300 - April 3, 1939.
"It appearing to the satisfaction of the court
that Sally Glassford, who was found an idiot
at a former term of this Court, still lives
and continues in the same situation, it is
therefore ordered to be certified to the Auditor
of Public Accounts that Andrew Zornes, the
committee of said Sally Glassford, is entitled
to receive at the rate of $50.00 per annum
from the 3rd day of April, 1838, to the 3rd
day of April, 1839, for the use and support
of said Sally Glassford."

Griffith, Mary:
38/213 - November 6, 1897.
"It appearing to the satisfaction of the
Court that George Wurts, Amos Carr, Celia
Leathers, Lucy Middaugh, Minnie McGinnis, Did
Nicholls, Isaiah Stepter, John Traylor, Minta
Traylor, William Friley, and Mary Griffith,
idiots, and John Wood and Mary Wheeler,
lunatics, are still alive, in the care of their
committees and have not sufficient estate for
their support, and that their parents are still
unable to support them, it is ordered that
the allowance of $75.00 each per annum for
their support be continued from the last payment
and that the same be copied and certified to
the Auditor for payment."

39/383 November 11, 1901.
"It appearing to the satisfaction of the
Court that Mary Wheeler and John Wood, lunatics,
and Amos Carr, Cynthia Ann Burton, Minta
Traylor, John Traylor, Lucy Middaugh, Did
Nicholls, Isaiah Stepter, Minnie McGinnis,
and Mary Griffith, idiots, are still alive,
in the care of their committees, and have not
estate sufficient for their support, and that
their parents are still unable to support them."

Guilkey, Grace (Gracie):
37/260 - July 17, 1894.
"An inquest was this day held upon Grace
Guilkey, an idiot, and recorded."

38/152 - July 20, 1897.

"W. M. Stevens appeared in Court and tendered
his resignation as committee for Gracie Guilkey,
an idiot, which is accepted. Ordered that
F. M. Warnock be appointed committee for said
idiot. He thereupon appeared in Court and
took the oath required by law, and together
with I. N. McGinnis, who is accepted and
approved by the Court, as his surety, executed
bond to the Commonwealth of Kentucky as committee aforesaid, conditioned according to
law."

39/368 - November 7, 1901.
"It appearing to the satisfaction of the
court that Gracie Guilkey, Hannah Davis, Ella
Jennings, Birdie Traylor, William C. Kitts,
James A. Kitts, Bennie Adkins, John Murphy,
and Martha Wadkins, idiots, are still alive,
in the care of their committees, and have not
sufficient estate for their support, and that
their parents are still unable to support them,
it is ordered that the allowance of $75.00
per annum each for their support be continued
from the last payment, and that the same be
copied and certified to the Auditor of Public
Accounts for payment."

Guy, Mary:
P/278 - April 24, 1850 (age 17).
"The said Mary Guy was brought into Court
by Benjamin Ulen, keeper of the poor house,
at which place the said Mary has been supported
for the last twelve months, and whereupon Benjamin F. King, David E. Poynter, Jesse Poynter,
Henry B. Pollard, Henry Williams, Charles
Barrett, Charles Craycraft, I. W. Gore, Truman
G. Waring, James Bayan, George W. Darlinton
and Hezekiah Morton were empanelled, sworn
and charged according to law as a jury of
inquest under the said writ, and having heard
the evidence returned the following verdict,
towit: 'We, the jury, find that said Mary
Guy is a lunatic and has been so for several
years, and that she has no estate of any kind;
that she is now about 17 years of age and has
no family; has been living in Greenup County
for the past 14 years; that her father is dead
and her mother resides in the State of Ohio;

that she can neither read, nor write; has no
relations known to the jury to be insane; no
particular illusion of the mind, and is quiet
and peaceable.'
     It is therefore considered by the court
that the said Mary Guy is a lunatic and that
she be taken to and confined in the lunatic
asylum at Lexington, there to remain until
discharged therefrom, and that Benjamin Ulen
be and he is hereby appointed to take charge
of said Mary Guy and convey her to the asylum
and deliver her to the officers of the same."

Hacket, John:
T/252 - May 14, 1858.
     "It being suggested to the court by A. C.
VanDyke that John Hacket is of unsound mind
and running at large. It is therefore ordered
that the Sheriff of this county apprehend the
said John Hacket and the said Hacket being
brought into court.
     Upon Motion of the attorney for the Common-
wealth it is ordered that a Writ of Deidiota
inqirendo issue returnable immediately to
inquire into the state of mind of the said
John Hacket, and it is further ordered that
L. W. Andrews, Esq., be appointed counsel for
the said John Hackett, and thereupon a jury,
to-wit: Jefferson Keeton, Reuben T. Thompson,
Thaddius Bennett, Wm. Jones, Wm. H. Lampton,
John Clifton, Wm. Hampton, David D. Geiger,
John N. Bates, Thomas Tudor and Charles Kinner,
who being sworn according to law upon their
oath returned the following verdict, to-wit:
'We, the jury, being sworn and impanelled to
inquire into the condition of the mind and
estate of John Hacket, and having had a view
of the said Hacket in open court, and having
other evidence as to his mind, do find said
Hacket to be a lunatic, has no estate, no local
habitation or residence, is a German by birth
and was found wandering about the highways
of the County of Greenup and laboring under
mental derangement. That he has no relatives
as far as the jury has been informed.' (signed)
Jefferson Keeton, Reuben T. Thompson, Thaddius
Bennett, William Jones, Wm. A. Lampton, John
Clifton, Wm. Hampton, David D. Geiger, John

Bates, Thomas Tudor, Charles Kinner, James
Rouse.
   And the court being satisfied with the
inquest adjudges that said John Hackett is
a lunatic, according to the finding of the
Jury, and the Court being of the opinion that
it would be unsafe to let said Hackett run
at large, it is ordered that he be confined
to the Jail of Greenup County."

Halstead, Henry H.:
34/22- March 2, 1882 (age 41).
   "Upon motion of the attorney for the Commonwealth, it is ordered that a Writ inquirendo
issue in the case of Henry H. Halstead, a
lunatic, returnable immediately, to inquire
into the state of mind of said Henry H.
Halstead, and it is ordered that Jeremiah Davidson, Esq., be appointed counsel for said Henry
H. Halstead. Whereupon came a jury, towit:
C_____ Firts, Moses Pickens, Clem Swearingen,
John W. Collins, Frank Meadows, William Lee,
Robert Roe, P. McClery, William Malone, William
Biggs, John T. King and John L. McAllister,
who being sworn according to law, returned
the following verdict, towit: 'We, the jury,
impaneled and sworn under a writ from the
Greenup Circuit Court directing us to inquire
if Henry H. Halstead of Greenup County be of
unsound mind, and having had a view of said
Halstead in open court, and having had evidence
in relation to his mind as well as estate,
do find that Henry H. Halstead is a lunatic;
is about 41 years of age; and that he has no
estate of his own; that he resides with his
wife, who has not sufficient estate for one
year's maintenance of said Halstead; that he
was born in Virginia; that he was not destitute
of mind from infancy, and that he was not
brought into the state by any person for the
purpose of becoming a charge upon the Commonwealth, and that he is incapable of laboring
for his own support in whole or in part. Given
under our hands and seals this 2nd day of March,
1882. (signed) J. W. Collins.
   Wherefore it is adjudged by the court that
said Henry H. Halstead is a lunatic, and that
he be taken by the Sheriff of Greenup County

to one of the lunatic asylums for the State
of Kentucky."

34/28 - March 3, 1882.
"The condition of the lunatic requiring,
ordered that the Sheriff summon two guards
to aid him in conveying said lunatic to the
Asylum."

34/31 - March 4, 1882.
"Upon motion of the attorney for the Commonwealth, it is ordered that a Writ of de lunde
(sic) inquirendo issue in the case of Henry
H. Halstead, a lunatic, returnable immediately,
to inquire into the state of mind of said Henry
H. Halstead."

34/60 - September 1, 1882 (age 40).
"We, the jury, impaneled and sworn under a
writ from the Greenup Circuit Court directing
us to inquire if Henry Halstead be of unsound
mind, and having had a view of said Henry
Halstead in open Court, and having had evidence
that said Henry Halstead is a lunatic, is about
40 years of age, and has no estate either in
possession, reversion or remainder; that he
resides in the poorhouse Greenup County, that
he was born in Virginia; that he has lost his
mind since his birth, and that he was not
brought into this state by any person for the
purpose of becoming a charge upon the Commonwealth, and that he is incapable of laboring
in whole or in part for his support; that he
has heretofore been found a lunatic. It is
therefore considered that said Henry Halstead
be allowed at the rate of $75.00 per annum
to clothe and maintain him, payable to his
committee. Ordered B. F. Brown be appointed
his committee."

34/87 - March 1, 1883.
"It appearing to the satisfaction of the
Court that Henry Halstead, a lunatic, was alive
up to the 15 day of November 1882, and in the
care of his committee, and was unable to labor
in whole or in part for his support, and that
his parents are still unable to support him,
it is ordered that the allowance of $75.00

per annum be continued from the inquest of
the Jury herein to the 15th day of November
1882, which is ordered to be certified to the
Auditor for payment."

"It appearing to the satisfaction of the
Court that Henry Halstead, a lunatic, died
on the 15th day of November 1882, it is ordered
that B. F. Brown, his committee, be allowed
$10.00 to defray expenses of the burial of
said lunatic, which is ordered to be copied
and certified to the Auditor for payment."

34/117 - March 9, 1883.
"Upon proof being made to the satisfaction
of the Court that Henry Halstead, heretofore
found to be a lunatic and confined in the asylum
until he was returned to Greenup upon the 17th
day of April 1882, was alive at the August
term 1882 of the Greenup Circuit Court and
was still a lunatic, and had not sufficient
estate for his support, and that his parents
were unable to support him, and that he had
been kept, clothed, and maintained by the
Greenup County Court from said 17 day of April
1882 to the August term 1882, it is ordered
by the Court that Greenup County and its
treasurer be allowed at the rate of $75.00
per annum from the 17th day of April 1882 to
the appointment of B. F. Brown as committee
at the August term 1882 of the Greenup Circuit
Court, which is ordered to be certified to
the Auditor of Public Accounts for payment."

Ham, Caroline:
38/178 - July 23, 1897.
"An inquest was this day held upon Caroline
Ham, an idiot, and recorded."

39/372 - November 8, 1901.
"It appearing to the satisfaction of the
court that Martha Jasper and Mary Clutts,
lunatics, and John Lawson, Christina McFarland,
William Vandergriff, Caroline Ham, Cora Horner,
Lavinia Flannigan, idiots, are still alive,
in the care of their committees and have not
estate sufficient for their support, and that
their parents are still unable to support them,

it is ordered that the allowance of $75.00
per annum each for their support be continued
from the last payment, and that the same be
copied and certified to the Auditor of Public
Accounts for payment."

Hensley, Matt B.:
35/86 - August 24, 1885.
   "The proceeding of the Boyd Circuit Court
in the case of Matt B. Hensley was this day
filed.
   Ordered that H. M. Rye be appointed a committee to take charge of said Matt B. Hensley
and provide him with suitable diet, clothing,
etc. Whereupon he appeared in Court and with
J. S. Hern as his surety, who is accepted and
approved by the Court, executed bond as committee aforesaid, conditioned according to
law. Upon proof being made to the satisfaction
of the Court that Matt B. Hensley heretofore
found to be a lunatic, is still alive, in the
care of his committee, and has not sufficient
estate for his support and that his parents
are still unable to support him, it is ordered
that H. M. Rye, his committee, be allowed at
the rate of $75.00 per annum for his support
from the order of the Boyd Circuit Court at
its October term 1883 to this date, which is
ordered to be certified to the Auditor of Public
Accounts."

35/208 - August 23, 1886.
   "Upon motion of H. M. Rye, it is ordered
that he be released from further duty as committee; ordered that B. F. Brown be appointed
committee for said Matt Hensley. Whereupon
he appeared in court and took the oath required
by law, and with J. Watt Womack as his surety,
who is accepted and approved by the Court,
executed bond as committee aforesaid, conditioned according to law."

   "It appearing to the satisfaction of the
court that Matt Hensley, a lunatic, is still
alive, in the care of his committee and has
not sufficient estate for his support, and
his parents are still unable to support him,
it is ordered that the allowance of $75.00

per annum be continued from last payment and
the same certified to the Auditor for payment.
   Upon motion of H. M. Rye, it is ordered
that he be released from further duty as committee.
   Ordered that B. F. Brown be appointed committee for said Matt Hensley. Whereupon he
appeared in court and took the oath required
by law, and with J. Watt Womack as his security,
who is accepted and approved by the court,
executed bond as committee aforesaid, conditioned according to law."

36/176 - August 27, 1889.
   "It appearing to the satisfaction of the
court that Matt Hensley, a lunatic, was alive
and in the care of his committee up to the
10th day of August 1889, and had not sufficient
estate for his support and that his parents
were unable to support him, it is ordered that
the allowance of $75.00 per annum be continued
from the last payment up to the 10th day of
August 1889, and that the same be certified
to the Auditor of Public Accounts."

Hill, Thomas:
38/107 - April 6, 1897.
   "An inquest was this day held upon Thomas
Hill, an idiot, and recorded."

38/114 - April 8, 1897.
   "Ordered that I. N. McGinnis be removed as
committee for Thomas Hill, an idiot, and that
W. M. Stevens be appointed committee for said
idiot in place of said McGinnis."

39/232 - November 8, 1900.
   "It appearing to the satisfaction of the
court that Martha Jasper, a lunatic, and Sreany
Ferguson, James A. Kitts, William C. Kitts,
John Murphy, Bennie Adkins, Bertha Traylor,
Thomas Hill, Martha Wadkins, Christina McFarland
and Hannah Davis, idiots, and Mary Clutts,
a lunatic, are still alive, in the care of
their committees, and have not sufficient estate
for their support, and that their parents are
still unable to suport them, it is ordered
that the allowance of $75.00 per annum each

for their support be continued from the last
payment, and that the same be copied and certified to the Auditor of Public Accounts for
payment."

39/337 - July 17, 1901.
    "Thomas Hill, an idiot, having removed from
Greenup County, it is ordered that the allowance
of $75.00 per annum for his support be continued
from the last payment until the first day of
July 1901, which is ordered to be copied and
certified to the Auditor of Public Accounts
for payment."

Hoffman, William:
T/340 - May 22, 1858.
    "It being suggest to the Court that William
Hoffman is of unsound mind and running at large,
it is ordered that the Sheriff of Greenup County
arrest the said Hoffman and deliver him to
the Jailer of the Greenup County who is required
to confine him until the further (Order) of
this court."

Horner, Cora:
38/393 - November 10, 1898.
    "It appearing to the satisfaction of the
court, upon proof heard, that Mary Wheeler
and John Wood, lunatics, and Cynthia A. Burton,
Amos Carr, William Friley, Mary Griffith, Celia
Leathers, Minnie McGinnis, Lucy Middaugh, Did
Nicholls, John Traylor, Mintie Traylor, Isaiah
Stepter, James Burriss, George Wurts, Hannah
Davis, John Davis, Cora Horner and Caroline
Ham, idiots, are still alive, in the care of
their committees and have not sufficient estate
for their support, and that their parents are
still unable to support them, it is ordered
that the allowance of $75.00 per annum each
for their support be continued from the last
payment, and that the same be copied and certified to the Auditor of Public Accounts for
payment."

39/372- November 8, 1901.
    "It appearing to the satisfaction of the
court that Martha Jasper and Mary Clutts, lunatics, and John Lawson, Christina McFarland,

William Vandergriff, Caroline Ham, Cora Horner,
Lavinia Flannigan, idiots, are still alive,
in the care of their committees and have not
estate sufficient for their support, and that
their parents are still unable to support them,
it is ordered that the allowance of $75.00
per annum each for their support be continued
from the last payment, and that the same be
copied and certified to the Auditor of Public
Accounts for payment."

Hyden, Allen:
35/470 - March 8, 1888 (age 35).
    "This day the attorney for the Commonwealth
filed an information as follows: To Hon. F.
B. Trussell, Special Judge of the Greenup
Circuit Court, I am reliably informed that
Allen Hyden is a person of unsound mind and
a lunatic, and therefore ask that a jury be
impaneled to pass upon the subject. (signed)
B. E. Roe, County Attorney, Greenup County.
    Ordered by the Court that J. B. Bennett,
Esq., an attorney of this Court, be and he
is hereby appointed to defend for and on behalf
of the person under trial. To inquire comes
a jury towit: T. J. Wilson, J. F. Taylor,
John Collins, Thomas McKee, A. J. Sennett,
Harrison Biggs, W. H. Clifton, Matthew Warnock,
Leander Martin, A. B. Morton, Jacob Urban and
Jacob Collins, who being duly elected and sworn
according to law, after hearing the evidence,
returned the following verdict, viz: 'We of
the jury find from the evidence that Allen
Hyden is a person of unsound mind and a lunatic;
that the unsoundness of mind has existed for
some three years, cause supposed to be from
sunstroke and spinal affection; that he was
born in Boyd County, and resides in Greenup
County, Kentucky, and is 35 years old; that
he was not brought into this State for the
purpose of becoming a charge upon the Commonwealth; that he owns no estate of any kind;
that his father is dead and mother dead and
said lunatic is not capable of laboring in
whole or in part for his support.' (signed)
A. B. Morton, Foreman
    It is therefore considered that said Allen
Hyden is a lunatic and that he be conveyed

to the State Lunatic Asylum at Lexington,
Kentucky, and that John T. Womack, Deputy
Sheriff, take charge of said Lunatic and convey
him to said Asylum; and that the be allowed
one guard to assist him."

Ingraham (Ingram), Rosetta:
S/93 - May 26, 1856 (age 25).
    "On motion of the attorney for the Common-
wealth, it is ordered that a Writ of De Idiota
Inquirendo issue in the case of Rosetta
Ingraham, a lunatic, returnable immediately,
to inquire into the state of mind of the said
Rosetta Ingraham, and it is ordered that William
Ireland, Esq., be appointed counsel for said
Rosetta Ingraham. Whereupon came a jury, towit:
Alex Rankins, O. F. MacKoy, Benj. F. King,
Reuben Thompson, William Bryson, Henry Ribble,
Thomas I. Poteet, Cyrus VanBibber, Aaron B.
Bush, William Littlejohn, John Brown and Moses
F. Dupuy, who being sworn according to law
returned the following verdict, towit: 'Having
heard the evidence of witnesses and having
a view of said Rosetta in open court, we, the
jury, find said Rosetta Ingram to be a lunatic,
that she is the wife of John Ingram, 25 years
of age, has been married 5 years, is the mother
of 3 children, the youngest of whom is 6 weeks
old, that her insanity commenced about one
week after the birth of her last child and
caused by the perpereal fever; that her husband
as not sufficient estate to maintain the said
Rosetta; that the said Rosetta has no estate
of her own; that she resides with her husband
in Greenup County.' (signed) Alexander Rankins,
O. F. McCoy, Ben F. King, Reuben Thompson,
William Bryson, Henry Ribble, Thos. I. Poteet,
Cyrus VanBibber, Aaron B. Bush, Wm. Littlejohn,
John Brown, M. F. Dupuy
    In this case it appearing from the evidence
and from certificates of attending physicians
not read to the jury that the Defendant, Rosetta
Ingram about the 13th of April 1856 was confined
(childbirth), at that time she was sane and
general health good. Some 3 or 4 days after
the 13th she took cold which resulted in fever,
at this point the first alienation of mind
commenced. She had been married 5 years and

has 3 children, the youngest 6 weeks old. She
is 25 years of age. There appears to be no
one of the family of the Defendant in any way
insane. There appear to be no one subject on
which she is deranged. Her general health has
in great measure been restored. (signed) W.
S. Botts, Circuit Judge."

S/95 - May 27, 1856.
  "It is ordered that John Ingram, husband
of Rosetta Ingram, to conduct her to Kentucky
Lunatic Asylum at Lexington and deliver her
into the keep of the Superintendent thereof."

Jacobs, Mary:
37/414 - July 19, 1895.
  "Lucy Smith, Amanda Smith, Jennie Smith,
Mary Hill and Samuel S. Smith filed a Petition
herein alleging that Mary Jacobs is a person
of unsound mind and incapable of managing her
estate, and moved the Court to issue a Writ
De Lunatic Inquiredo to inquire to the state
of mind of said Mary Jacobs as well as her
estate and appoint a committee to take charge
of the person and estate of said Mary Jacobs,
and the same is submitted upon said motion."

Jameson, George W.:
29/252 - March 19, 1874.
It appearing to the satisfaction of the court
that George W. Jameson, a pauper lunatic, was
confined in the Greenup County Jail in the
custody and control of Charles Callihan, Jailer
for Greenup County, as his committee, and had
not sufficient estate for his support, and
no friends or parents able to support him,
and that said pauper lunatic was taken care
of by said Jailer Callihan from the ____ day
of _____ 1873, until the ____ day of
_____ 1873, making 137 days.
  It is therefore ordered that the allowance
at the rate of $200.00 per annum be paid to
said Callihan for the porportionable time he
kept said pauper lunatic, which amounts to
the sum of $75.06, and that the same be certi-
fied to the Auditor for payment under the Act
approved March 28, 1872."

Jamison, George:
29/251 - March 19, 1874.
   "It appearing to the satisfaction of the
court that George Jamison, a pauper lunatic,
was confined in the Greenup County Jail in
the custody and control of James P. Winter,
Jailer of Greenup County, as his committee,
and had not sufficient estate for his support
and no friends or parents to support him, and
that said pauper lunatic was taken care of
by said Jailer Winter from the 13th day of
August 1873, until the 15th day of October
1873, viz 64 days.
   It is therefore ordered that the allowance
at the rate of $200.00 per annum be paid said
Winters for the porportionable time he kept
said pauper lunatic which amounts to the sum
of $35.06, and that the same be certified to
the Auditor for payment under the Act approved
March 28, 1872."

Jamison, John:
36/231 - February 24, 1890.
"It appearing to the satisfaction of the court
that Cynthia Burton, John Jamison, John Davis,
Robert Davis, idiots, and Mary Clutz and Martha
Jasper, lunatics, are still alive and in the
care of their committee, and have not sufficient
estate for their support, and that their parents
are unable to support them, it is ordered that
the allowance of $75.00 per annum be continued
from the last payment and that the same be
copied and certified to the Auditor of Public
Accounts."

37/7 - August 23, 1892.
   "It appearing to the satisfaction of the
court that James A. Kitts, John Jamisen, idiots,
and Martha Jasper, a lunatic, are still alive
and in the care of their committee, and have
not sufficient estate for their support, and
that their parents are still unable to support
them, it is ordered that the allowance of $75.00
per annum be continued from the last payment,
and that the same be certified to the Auditor
of Public Accounts."

Jamison (Jameison), John R.:

36/4 - August 28, 1888.

"It appearing to the satisfaction of the court that Mary Clutz, Martha Jasper, and Matt Hensley, lunatics, and Celia Leathers, John Murphy, Did Nicholls, Cynthia Burton, Jacob Steenrod, Grant Damarin, George Wurts, and James A. Kitts, John R. Jamison and Magdalena Gonae, idiots, are still alive, in the care of their committees, and have not sufficient estate for their support, and that their parents are still unable to support them, it is ordered that the allowance of $75.00 each per annum be continued them from the last payment, which is ordered to be copied and certified to the Auditor for payment."

NOTE: I believe this is probably John T. Jamison as John R. Jamison was committee for John T. Jamison and this is the only entry for a John R. Jamison as a person under trial.

Jamison (Jameison, Jamisen, Jamesin), John T.: 35/445 - March 1, 1888 (age 24).

"This day the attorney for the Commonwealth filed an information as follows: to-wit, To Hon. F. B. Trussell, Special Judge of the Greenup Circuit Court: I am reliably informed that John T. Jamisen is a person of unsound mind and an idiot, and therefore ask that a jury be impanelled to pass upon the subject. (signed) James H. Sallee, Commonwealth Attorney, 14th Judicial District.

'We, the jury, find from the evidence that John T. Jamesin is a person of unsound mind, and an idiot, that the unsoundness of mind has existed from birth; that he was born in Greenup County, and resides in Greenup County, and is 24 years old; that he was not brought into this state for the purpose of becoming a charge upon the Commonwealth; that he owns no estate of any kind; that his father is living and mother living and resides in Greenup County, Kentucky, and they have not estate sufficient to support the person under trial, and said idiot is not capable of laboring in whole or in part for his support.' (signed) Thomas M. Hebeerlin, foreman.

It is therefore ordered that John R. Jamesin be appointed a committee to take charge of

said John T. Jamesin and provide with suitable
diet, clothing, etc., and that he be allowed
therefor at the rate of $75.00 per annum from
this date, to be paid upon the further Orders
of this Court. The said John R. Jamesin thereupon appeared in Court and with James Logan
as his security, who is accepted and approved
by the Court, executed bond to the Commonwealth of Kentucky as committee condition
according to law, all of which is ordered to
be copied and certified to the Auditor of Public
Accounts."

37/92 - April 6, 1893.
    "It appearing to the satisfaction of the
Court that John T. Jameison, an idiot, was
alive up to the 25th day of February 1893,
and had not sufficient estate for his support,
and that his parents were unable to support
him, it is ordered that the allowance of $75.00
per annum be continued from the last payment
up to the 25th day of February 1893, the date
of the death of Jameison, and that the same
be certified to the Auditor for payment."

Jasper, Martha A.:
35/6 - February 23, 1885.
    "A copy of the inquest and the certificate
of the Medical Superintendent and Board of
Commissioners of the Eastern Kentucky Lunatic
Asylum at Lexington, Kentucky, was this day
filed in the case of Martha Jasper, a lunatic,
and it appearing to the satisfaction of the
Court that Martha Jasper, a lunatic, is still
alive and has been in the care of Thomas Jasper
since removed from said Asylum; and that she
has not sufficient estate for her support and
that her parents are unable to support her,
it is therefore ordered that there be allowed
for her support at the rate of $75.00 per annum
from the 27th day of September 1884, the time
of her removal from the Asylum."

35/15 - February 24, 1885.
    "Ordered that Thomas Jasper be appointed
a committee to take charge of and provide the
said Martha Jasper with suitable food and
raiment (sic) and to provide for and maintain

the said Martha in a suitable manner. He thereupon appeared in Court and with David Sullivan
his surety, who is accepted and approved by
the Court, executed bond as committee aforesaid,
conditioned according to law."

35/97 - August 25, 1885.
    "It appearing to the satisfaction of the
Court that Martha Jasper, a lunatic, is still
alive, in the care of her committee, and has
not sufficient estate for her support, and
that her parents are still unable to support
her, it is ordered that the allowance of $75.00
per annum be continued from the last payment,
and that the same be certified to the Auditor."

39/372 - November 8, 1901.
"Inquests were this day held upon Martha Jasper,
a lunatic, and John Lawson and Mary Griffith,
idiots, and recorded."

Jennings, Ella:
37/302 - November 8, 1894.
    "It appearing to the satisfaction of the
court that Mary Wheeler and John Wood, lunatics,
and James A. Kitts, William C. Kitts, Ella
Jennings, Amos Carr, Isaiah Stepter, Celia
Leathers, Did Nicholls, Grant Damarin and Lucy
Middaugh, idiots, are still alive, in the care
of their respective committees, and have not
sufficient estate for their support, and that
their parents are still unable to support them,
it is ordered that the allowance of $75.00
per annum be continued from the last payment,
and that the same be certified to the Auditor
for payment."

39/368 - November 7, 1901.
    "It appearing to the satisfaction of the
court that Gracie Guilkey, Hannah Davis, Ella
Jennings, Birdie Traylor, William C. Kitts,
James A. Kitts, Bennie Adkins, John Murphy,
and Martha Wadkins, idiots, are still alive,
in the care of their committees, and have not
sufficient estate for their support, and that
their parents are still unable to support them,
it is ordered that the allowance of $75.00
per annum each for their support be continued

from the last payment, and that the same be
copied and certified to the Auditor of Public
Accounts for payment."

Kilburn, Aepheus:
36/294 - August 25, 1890.
   "The proceedings before the Greenup County
Court, by which Aepheus Kilburn was adjudged
a lunatic, was this day produced and filed,
and it appearing to the satisfaction of the
Court that the said Aepheus Kilburn is a lunatic
and is still alive, and has not sufficient
estate for his support, and that his parents
are still unable to support him, it is ordered
that J. Watt Womack be appointed a committee
to take charge of said Aepheus Kilburn and
provide him with suitable diet, clothing, etc.,
and that he be allowed therefor at the rate
of $75.00 per annum, to be paid upon the fur-
ther orders of this court.
   And it further appearing that said Aepheus
Kilburn is and was a harmless lunatic, and
that admittance was refused in the Lunatic
Asylum of the State because he was a harmless
lunatic, and that J. Watt Womack has kept and
provided the said Aepheus Kilburn with suitable
diet, clothing, etc. from the 13th day of May
1890, the date of refusal to receive him in
said asylum, it is ordered that he be allowed
at the rate of $75.00 per annum therefor from
the 13th day of May 1890, and that same be
copied and certified to the Auditor for
payment."

36/314 - August 27, 1890.
   "J. Watt Womack, committee for Aepheus
Kilburn, this day came into court and with
John T. Womack as his surety, who is accepted
and approved by the Court, executed bond to
the Commonwealth of Kentucky as committee aforesaid
conditioned according to law."

36/473 - February 23, 1892.
   "It appearing to the satisfaction of the
Court that Aepheus Kilburn, a lunatic, was
alive and in the care of J. W. Womack, his
committee, up to the 10th day of December 1891,
when he died, and had not sufficient estate

for his support, and that his parents were
unable to support him, it is ordered that the
allowance of $75.00 per annum be continued
from the last payment up to the death of said
Kilburn, December 10, 1891, and that the same
be certified to the Auditor of Public Accounts.

It appearing to the satisfaction of the
Court that Aepheus Kilburn, a lunatic, died
on the 10th day of December 1891, and that
J. Watt Womack, his committee, expended $10.00
for his burial expenses, it is ordered that
said J. Watt Womack, committee of said Kilburn,
be allowed $10.00, the burial expenses of said
Kilburn, and that same be certified to the
Auditor for payment."

Kitts, James A.:
35/164 - February 24, 1886 (age 14).
"On motion of the Commonwealth, it is ordered
that a Writ of de idota inquirendo issue in
the case of James A. Kitts, an idiot, returnable
immediately, to inquire into the state of mind
of said Kitts, and it is ordered that D. J.
McCoy be appointed counsel for said Kitts.
Whereupon came a jury: Stephen Lozier, Charles
Smith, L. P. Harrisen, Geo. W. Robinsen, O.
D. Riffe, D. S. Mitchell, R. F. Dingess, John
Patton, Arch Conway, John Riggs, James Burkley,
and Hamilton Walker, who being sworn according
to law returned the following verdict: 'We,
the jury, find from the evidence that James
A. Kitts is a person of unsound mind and an
idiot; that the unsoundness of mind has existed
from birth; that he was born in Greenup County,
Kentucky, and resides in Greenup County,
Kentucky, and is 14 years old; that he was
not brought into this state for the purpose
of becoming a charge upon the Commonwealth;
that his father is living and mother is living
and residing in Greenup County, Kentucky, and
they have not estate sufficient to support
the person under trial, and said James A. Kitts
is not capable of laboring in whole or in part
for his support.' (signed) John Riggs, foreman.

It is therefore ordered that Chris Kitts
be appointed a committee to take charge of
said James A. Kitts and provide him with suitable diet, clothing, etc. and that he be

allowed therefor at the rate of $75.00 per
annum from this date, to be paid upon the further Order of this court. The said James A.
Kitts and Chris Kitts, committee as aforesaid,
appeared in court and with D. J. McCoy as his
surety, who is accepted and approved by the
Court, executed bond, conditioned according
to law."

39/368 - November 7, 1901.
"It appearing to the satisfaction of the
Court that Gracie Guilkey, Hannah Davis, Ella
Jennings, Birdie Traylor, William C. Kitts,
James A. Kitts, Bennie Adkins, John Murphy,
and Martha Wadkins, idiots, are still alive,
in the care of their committees and have not
sufficient estate for their support, and that
their parents are still unable to support them,
it is ordered that the allowance of $75.00
per annum each for their support be continued
from the last payment, and that the same be
copied and certified to the Auditor of Public
Accounts for payment."

Kitts, William C.:
37/202 - April 3, 1894.
"An inquest was this day held upon William
C. Kitts, an idiot, and recorded."

39/368 - November 7, 1901.
"It appearing to the satisfaction of the
Court that Gracie Guilkey, Hannah Davis, Ella
Jennings, Birdie Traylor, William C. Kitts,
James A. Kitts, Bennie Adkins, John Murphy,
and Martha Wadkins, idiots, are still alive,
in the care of their committees and have not
sufficient estate for their support, and that
their parents are still unable to support them,
it is ordered that the allowance of $75.00
per annum each for their support be continued
from the last payment, and that the same be
copied and certified to the Auditor of Public
Accounts for payment."

Lacey, Margaret: (sister of Aaron Tufts).
Q/38 - November 17, 1851 (age 26).
"Upon motion of the attorney for the Common-
wealth, who represents that Mrs. John Lacey

of this County is a person of unsound mind,
it is ordered that a writ of de luniatico
inquirendo issue for the purpose of inquiring
into the state of mind of the said Mrs. John
Lacey, and whether she hath any estate and,
if any, the nature and extent thereof, and
Leander M. Cox is appointed counsel for the
said Mrs. John Lacey. Whereupon the said writ
having issued and being returned executed and
the jury summoned, viz: Jerimiah Farmer, Jesse
Poynter, I. K. Poynter, B. F. Lawson, Charles
Crooks, Jackson H. Jacobs, Moses F. Dupuy,
William H. Warnoch, John C. Feirink, Matthew
Warnoch, R. T. Thompson, and A. J. Bushby were
sworn and charged to inquire and having heard
the evidence returned the following verdict,
viz: 'We, the jury, find that said Mrs. John
Lacey is a person of unsound mind and a lunatic,
26 years of age, a married woman, has three
children; that she has been a lunatic for two
years, the first attack of was about two years
since the symptoms first exhibited themselves
as in a case of idiocy and has not changed
in the character of the lunacy but has decreased
in degree. There are no peculiar illusions.
She has never attempted to commit suicide;
is not subject to fits; the cause of insanity
is not known to the jurors. Her father was
insane and a brother and sister are insane.
Her disposition is mild, has but a moderate
education, and her general health is good.
She is the wife of John Lacey, who is not worth
more than $300.00 in property and labors for
his own support and for the support of his
family and has not sufficient estate to maintain
the said Margaret Lacey in her present condition. The said Margaret Lacey has resided
in Greenup County from her birth. It is therefore considered by the Court that said Margaret
Lacey is a lunatic and that she be taken to
and confined in the Lunatic Asylum at Lexington,
there to remain until discharged therefrom.'"
    NOTE: 6/52 - June 1, 1857 - Wealthy Ann
Tuffs appointed guardian of John W. Lacey,
Mary H. Lacey and Marvin V. Lacey, infant
orphans of John Lacy. (Wealthy Ann Tuffs,
Mother of Margaret Lacey).

Lands, Anna:
38/330 - July 22, 1898.
"An inquest was this day held on Anna Lands, a lunatic, and recorded."

Lawson, John:
38/84 - November 10, 1896.
"An inquest was this day held upon John Lawson, a lunatic, and recorded."

39/372 - November 8, 1901.
"Inquests were this day held upon Martha Jasper, a lunatic, and John Lawson and Mary Griffith, idiots, and recorded."

Leathers, Celia:
35/284 - March 2, 1887 (age 8).
"Upon motion of the attorney for the Commonwealth, it is ordered that a writ de idiota inquirendo issue in the case of Celia Leathers, an idiot, returnable immediately, to inquire into the state of mind of said Leathers, and it is ordered that B. F. Bennett, Esq., be appointed counsel for said Leathers, whereupon came a jury, towit: Charles Stewart, John Goad, E. G. Warnock, Thomas Abrams, T. M. Heberlin, W. A. Simonton, G. W. Truett, James H. Logan, H. C. Morton, H. G. Grant, J. W. Greenslate and James Gholstin, who being sworn according to law returned the following verdict: 'We, the jury, find from the evidence that Celia Leathers is a person of unsound mind and an idiot; that the unsoundness of mind has existed from infancy; that she was born in Greenup in May 1878 and resides in Greenup County, and is 8 years old; that she was not brought into this County for the purpose of becoming a charge upon the Commonwealth; that she owns no estate of any kind; that her father is living and mother living and reside in Greenup County, and they have not sufficient to support the person under trial, and said idiot is not capable of laboring in whole or part for her support.' (signed) H. C. Morton, foreman.
It is therefore ordered that B. F. Brown be appointed a committee to take charge of said Celia Leathers and provide her with suffi-

cient diet, clothing, etc., and that he be
allowed therefor at the rate of $75.00 per
annum from this date to be paid upon the further
order of the Court."

39/385 - November 11, 1901.
"It appearing to the satisfaction of the
Court that Celia Leathers, an idiot, was alive
in the 21st day of April 1901, and had not
estate sufficient for her support, and that
her parents were still unable to support her,
and that said Celia Leathers died in said 21st
day of April 1901, it is ordered that the allowance of $75.00 per annum for her support be
continued from the last payment until and
including said 21st day of April 1901, and
that the same be copied and certified to the
Auditor of Public Accounts for payment."

Lewis, Alexander:
X/202 - September 6, 1864.
"This day came the attorney for the Commonwealth, and the Defendant (Alexander Lewis)
being brought to the bar in the custody of
the Jailer and being unable to employ counsel,
the Court required William C. Ireland, Esq.,
a member of this Bar, to act as counsel for
said Defendant, who agreed to act as such,
and thereupon the said Defendant plead not
guilty and the attorney for the Commonwealth
joined issue and thereupon came a jury, towit:
Moses F. Dupuy, Edward Brooks, Robert
McAllister, Samuel Ritzer, John Kout, James
Y. Pugh, Zachariah Richards, Robert Bradshaw,
James Clifton, John S. Crossett, Charles
Callihan and Clem Swearingen, who being elected,
tried and sworn well and truly to try the issue
joined and the evidence being heard, it is
on motion of the attorney for the Commonwealth
that the jury be discharged, and with the assent
of the court a Nolle Prosegni is entered herein.
And on Motion of the attorney for the Commonwealth it is ordered that a Writ of De-Idiota
Inquirendo issue to inquire into the state
of mind of the said Alexander Lewis, and William
C. Ireland, Esq., is appointed to defend the
said Alexander Lewis, and being present he
accepted said appointment, and the said

Alexander Lewis being in the presence of the
Court and of the jury, who are as follows:
Moses F. Dupuy, Edward Brooks, Robert
McAllister, Samuel Ritzer, John Kout, James
Y. Pugh, Zachariah Richards, Robert Bradshaw,
James Clifton, John S. Crossett, Charles
Callihan and Clem Swearingen, who being sworn
according to law returned the following verdict:
'We, the jury, find that Alexander Lewis is
of unsound mind; that he is a lunatic, having
lost his mind since his birth by reason of
wounds inflicted on his head some 9 years ago.
That he was born in Monro County, Virginia,
and came to Kentucky some 15 years ago; that
he has not been brought into this state by
any person for the purpose of becoming a charge
upon the Commonwealth. That he has no estate
in possession, reversion or remainder. His
parents are not alive. He is not capable of
laboring in part for his support.' (signed)
M. F. Dupuy, foreman
   And the court being satisfied with the
inquest adjudges that the said Alexander Lewis
is a lunatic, and that the other facts found
by the jury in their verdict are true, and
the Court being of opinion that it is unsafe
to let the said Lewis to run at large, orders
that he be remanded to the Jailer of this county
until such time as the Superintendent of the
Lunatic Asylum shall be notified of the finding
of the jury and the Judgment of the court in
this case."

Lyon(s), Jane:
33/346 - March 8, 1881.
   "Upon proof being made to the satisfaction
of the court that Jane Lyon, heretofore found
to be an idiot, is still alive, in the care
of her committee and has not sufficient estate
for her support, and that her parents are unable
to support her. It is ordered that the committee be allowed at the rate of $75.00 per
annum for her support, from the finding of
the jury, which is ordered to be certified
to the Auditor of Public Accounts for payment."

33/388 - March 17. 1881.

"Order that J. W. Kouns be appointed committee
for Jane Lyons to take charge of and provide
suitable diet, clothing, etc. Whereupon said
Kouns appeared in court and executed bond,
which is accepted and approved, as committee
aforesaid, conditioned according to law, which
is ordered to be copied and certified."

33/398 - August 22, 1881.
"Upon proof being made to the satisfaction
of the court that Jane Lyon heretofore found
to be an idiot, is still alive, in the care
of J. W. Kouns, her committee, and has not
sufficient estate for her support, and that
her parents are unable to support her, it is
ordered by the court that J. W. Kouns be allowed
at the rate of $75.00 per annum for her support,
from the finding of the jury at a former term
of this court to this date, which is ordered
to be certified to the Auditor of Public
Accounts for payment."

34/48 - August 30, 1882 (age 48).
"We, the jury, impaneled and sworn under
a Writ from the Greenup Circuit Court, directing
us to inquire if Jane Lyons of Greenup County
be of unsound mind, and having had evidence
in relation to the condition of her mind, she
not being in a condition to be brought into
court, as well as estate, do find that said
Jane Lyons is an idiot, is about 48 years old
and that she has not estate of her own, that
she resides with her mother, her father is
dead, who has not estate for one year's maintenance of said Jane Lyon; that she has no
estate in possession, remainder or reversion
sufficient to support her; that she was born
in Greenup County; that she was destitute of
mind from infancy; and that she was not brought
into the state by any person for the purpose
of becoming a charge upon the Commonwealth,
and that she is incapable of laboring for her
own support. (signed) Jacob Barney.
It is therefore ordered that there be allowed
to clothe, maintain and support said Jane Lyon
the sum of $75.00 per annum."

35/153 - February 23, 1886.

"It appearing to the satisfaction of the
Court that Jane Lyons, an idiot, was alive
upon the 4th day of February 1886, and in the
care of her committee, and had not sufficient
estate for her support and that her parents
were unable to support her, it is ordered that
the allowance for her support at the rate of
$75.00 per annum be continued from the last
payment to the 4th day of February 1886, when
said idiot died, and that same be copied and
certified to the Auditor of Public Accounts."

Martin, George W.:
34/167 - September 6, 1883.
"The parties appeared by their attorney and
thereupon came a jury, towit: John H. Warnock,
George Hager, Alfred Walker, Jasper Rake, Benjamin Smith, James Worthington, Basil Abrams,
Samuel Brown, Samuel Vallance, Jacob Rake,
R. Burkhardt, J. L. Bryson, who were duly sworn
and having heard the evidence returned the
following verdict: 'We, the jury, find George
Martin incompetent to control his own business
from mental incapacity.' (signed) J. L. Brysen.
    Wherefore, it is adjudged that George Martin
is incompetent to attend his own business from
mental incapacity and John W. Collins, his
former committee, declining to continue as
such, it is ordered that J. Watt Womack be
appointed as a committee to take charge of
his property."

36/110 - February 28, 1889.
"Ordered that Leander Martin be appointed
a committee for George W. Martin, an imbecile.
    He thereupon appeared in Court and took
the oath required by law, and with James D.
Biggs as his security, who is accepted and
approved by the Court, executed a bond to the
Commonwealth of Kentucky as committee aforesaid,
conditioned according to law."

McAllister, John:
Z/250 - December 3, 1868 (age 81).
"On Motion of the attorney for the Commonwealth it is ordered that a Writ of de idota
inquirendo issue in the case of John McCal-
lister, returnable immediately, to inquire

into the state of mind of said McAllister,
and it is orderd that ___(no name inserted)___
Esq., be appointed counsel for said McAllister,
whereupon came a jury towit: George W. Mead,
Thomas Roberts, Patrick Byrne, William Riley,
J. A. Brammer, Wm. Guthrie, Samuel Powell,
F. M. Huffman, Alexander Rankin, A. J. Sennett,
J. W. Davissen, Joseph Gray, who were duly
sworn and after hearing the evidence returned
the following verdict: 'We, the jury, find
John McAllister, the person whom we have in
charge, to be a person of unsound mind; that
his mind has commenced failing him within the
last two to three years, principally from old
age, he being 82 years old next March; he was
born in this State; he has sufficient estate
for his support; he is not capable of laboring
in whole or in part for his support; he has
a wife (being this third wife) now living with
him; he has several children by former wives
but none by his present wife; none of his
children live with him now; his wife has a
marriage contract entered into at the time
of their marriage.' (signed) James W. Davissen.
    It is therefore adjudged by the court that
the said John McAllister is a person of unsound
mind, and it is ordered that Henry J. McAllister
be appointed a committee to institute and
prosecute and defend all such suits or actions
which have been or may become necessary to
institute or defend for the preservation of
the estate of said John McAllister, and it
is further ordered that a Rule issue against
Sarah McAllister, wife of said John McAllister,
returnable to the next term, to show cause
why a committee shall not be appointed to take
charge of the estate of said John McAlister."

Z/281 - March 2, 1869 (age 82).
    "The matter of John McAllister, found to
be a person of unsound intellect: Sarah
McAllister filed her answer to the Rule heretofore ordered in this case. The court on con-
sideration of the matters now orders that Henry
J. McAllister be appointed committee for said
John McAllister, and that he be empowered in
not only to defend suits and to bring suits
where the interest of said John may require

it, but that he have the care and control of
all of his estate, and shall either permit
the said John and his family to use the same
or if necessary rent such parts of the realty
and sell such personal property, if any be
necessary, for the use of himself and family.
Shall out of the estate pay all just debts
against him and appropriate such part to his
support and to the support of his wife as shall
be necessary--having regard to the manner in
which said McAllister has heretofore lived.
He executed bond, with James McAllister as
his security, for proper discharge of his duties
under the laws of this state in such case
required and to perform the orders of the court,
which bond is approved by the court and ordered
to be filed. Said McAllister also in open
court took the oath required by law. He shall
report his acts to this court."

McFarland, Christina:
38/170 - July 22, 1897.
    "An inquest was this day held upon Christina
McFarland, and idiot, and recorded."

39/498 - July 23, 1902.
    "An inquest was this day held upon Christina
McFarland and recorded."

McGinnis, Minnie:
37/365 - April 5, 1895.
    "Inquests were this day held upon Minnie
McGinnis, Rebecca Traylor and John Traylor,
idiots, and recorded."

39/383 - November 11, 1901.
    "It appearing to the satisfaction of the
court that Mary Wheeler and John Wood, lunatics,
and Amos Carr, Cynthia Ann Burton, Minta
Traylor, John Traylor, Lucy Middaugh, Did
Nicholls, Isaiah Stepter, Minnie McGinnis,
and Mary Griffith, idiots, are still alive,
in the care of their committees, and have not
estate sufficient for their support, and that
their parents are still unable to support them."

McGuire, Martha:
37/342 - April 1, 1895.

"An inquest was this day held upon Martha
McGuire, a lunatic, and recorded.
Wherefore it is adjudged by the Court that
said Martha McGuire is a lunatic and Irvin
B. Hockaday is hereby appointed a committee
to convey said lunatic to the Eastern Asylum
at Lexington, Kentucky."

McKee, Elizabeth:
R/274 - May 28, 1855 (age 7).
"On motion of the attorney for the Commonwealth, who represents that he had been informed
that Elizabeth McKee of this county is a person
of unsound mind, it is ordered that a writ
of inquirendo de lunatico issue, returnable
immediately, to inquire into the state of mind
of the said Elizabeth McKee and whether she
has any estate, etc., and it is ordered that
Edward F. Dulin, Esq., be appointed counsel
for said Elizabeth McKee. Whereupon the said
Elizabeth McKee was brought into court, and
Charles Pearce, Alexander Davis, John C. Burk,
Carlisle Hunt, Jesse S. Dupuy, Richard Jones,
George Tanner, Thomas I. Poteet, Edward Brooks,
Benj. F. King, Nicholas Savage and John Hartley
were empannelled (sic), sworn and charged
according to law as a jury of inquest under
the said writ and having heard the evidence
returned the following verdict, towit: 'We,
the jury, find that Elizabeth McKee has been
an idiot from her birth; that she is 7 years
old; has a father and mother still living;
no relatives who have been insane; no cause
known of her idiotcy; no attempt at suicide;
no lucid intervals; frequent efforts have been
made to restore her; she has no estate. That
she has been found an idiot by a jury and Judgment of this Court on the _____ day of _____,
that no change has taken place in her condition
since the finding of the former jury, and that
no estate has come or descended to her since
that time, and that she is unable to perform
any labor, and that she has been in the County
of Greenup 7 years.' (signed) Charles Pearce,
Alexander Davis, John C. Burk, Carlisle Hunt,
Jesse S. Dupuy, Richard Jones, George Tanner,
Thomas J. Poteet, Edward Brooks, Benj. F. King,
Nicholas Savage, John Hartley.

It is, therefore, adjudged by the Court
that John McKee be appointed a committee to
take charge of the said Elizabeth McKee and
provide for her suitable diet, clothing, etc.,
and that he be allowed therefor at the rate
of $50.00 per annum from the last allowance
to be paid out of the treasury of this state,
which is ordered to be certified to the Auditor
of Public Accounts for payment."

V/235 - November 24, 1860 (age 15).
    "Upon motion of the attorney for the Common-
wealth, it is ordered that a Writ of de idota
inquirendo issue in the case of Elizabeth
Foster, an idiot, returnable immediately, to
inquire into the state of mind of the said
Elizabeth, and it is ordered that William C.
Ireland, Esq., be appointed counsel for said
Elizabeth. Whereupon the affidavits of Samuel
Ellis and A. D. Debord was produced to the
court, and it appearing from the said affidavits
that it is unsafe to cause said Elizabeth McKee
to be brought into court, the court orders
that her presence in court be dispensed with.
Whereupon came a jury, to wit: Clem Swearingen,
James Downs, George W. Smith, John W. Smith,
Jesse S. Dupuy, Samuel Powell, James Martin,
Benjamin King, S. H. Riggs, George W.
McAllister, James Davidson, and Benjamin Howland, who being sworn according to law,
returned the following verdict, to wit: 'We,
the jury, find that Elizabeth McKee is an idiot;
that she was born in Pennsylvania and is about
15 years of age, and has resided in this state
about 12 years; that she was not brought into
this state to become a charge upon the Commonwealth; that she has no property or estate
in possession, reversion, or remainder sufficient for her maintenance; her Father is dead,
but her Mother is alive and has not property
sufficient for the maintenance of said idiot.
We further find that the said Elizabeth McKee
has heretofore, by a verdict of a jury and
judgment of this court, been found an idiot,
and that no change has taken place in her mind,
physical condition, or estate since the finding
of the original inquest.' (signed) James Martin,
foreman.

And it is therefore ordered that Joseph
Pollock be appointed a committee to take charge
of said Elizabeth McKee and provide her with
suitable diet, clothing, etc., and that he
be allowed therefor at the rate of $50.00 per
annum from the last allowance, to be paid upon
the further order of this court. It is further
ordered that said Joseph Pollock give bond
and security in the penalty of $200.00 for
the faithful performance of his duty in this
case; and this day said Joseph Pollock with
William C. Ireland his security, (executed
bond) according to this order and the same
was accepted by the court and ordered to be
certified to the Auditor."

V/498 - May 26, 1862.
"It appearing to the satisfaction of the
Court that Elizabeth McKee, an idiot, departed
this life on the 19th day of March 1862, and
that she remained an idiot to the time of her
death; that she remainded in the care of her
committee; had not sufficient estate for her
support and that her parents were unable to
support her, it is ordered that the allowance
of $50.00 per annum be continued from the last
to the time of her death."

McKoy, Thomas:
P/93 - October 24, 1848.
"On motion of the attorney for the Commonwealth, who represents that Thomas McKoy of
this county is of unsound mind, it is ordered
that a writ of de lunatico inquiredo issue
for the purpose of inquiring into the state
of the mind of the said Thomas McKoy and whether
he has any estate, and if any the nature and
extent thereof, and L. W. Andrews, Esq., is
appointed counsel for the said Thomas McKoy.
Whereupon came a jury towit: Levi I. Hampton,
James Stewart, Nelson Jones, Basil Waring,
Rival D. Jones, James Osburn, William Waring,
James Sloan, Joshua L. Gammon, Archer Womack,
Wilson Lee and John Bell were sworn and charged
to inquire, etc. and having heard the evidence
returned the following verdict: 'We, the jury,
find that Thomas McKoy is a man without mind
sufficient to protect his own interests in

the management of his property, and therefore
we find him to be a man of unsound mind. We
further find that he is in possession of and
owns property sufficient for his support.'

It is therefore, considered by the court
that the said Thomas McKoy is an lunatic, and
that Moses McKoy and Benjamin F. King be and
are hereby appointed committee to take charge
of the person and estate of the said Thomas
McKoy and out of the rents, issues and profits
thereof provide for his comfortable support
and maintenance."

Middaugh, James Jr.:
X/251 - March 6, 1865 (age 22).
"On motion of the Commonwealth Attorney,
a jury was ordered to be impanelled and sworn
to inquire into the state of mind of James
Middaugh, Jr., the personal presence of said
James Middaugh, Jr., in court was dispensed
with on the investigation, it being legally
proven in court by Dr. Moore, a physician,
and others, that they have personally examined
the said Middaugh and that they verily believe
him to be a lunatic, and that his condition
is such that it would be unsafe to bring him
into court. That he is a raving maniac and
unmanageable and dangerous, and therefore came
a jury, viz: Reuben Thompson, John S. Hunt,
Eli Cooper, Lewis Hall, Alex Patton, Robert
McAlister, O. N. Jones, John Archey, O. F.
McKee, John Bagby, Saml Powell, and Charles
Callihan, who being duly sworn according to
law, after hearing the evidence and a charge
from the court, returned the following verdict:
'We, the jury, find that James Middaugh, Jr.,
which we have in charge, is a lunatic. He
lost his mind since his birth. We cannot say
from the evidence the cause of it, unless it
be over excitement and exposure. He is not
given to intoxication. He was born and always
resided in this county. He has no estate in
possession, reversion or remainder. His parents
are alive and live in this county, and they
have not estate sufficient to support him.
He is 22 years old last January. He is incapable of laboring in whole or in part for his
support. He first manifested signs of insanity

about six weeks or two months ago and for about
two weeks he has been a raving maniac, very
troublesome, unmanageable and dangerous.'
    Wherefore, it is adjudged by the court that
the said James Middaugh, Jr., is a lunatic,
and that the other facts found by the jury
in their verdict are true, and that he be taken
to the Lunatic Asylum. And Andrew O'Neal be
appointed a committee to take him to said
asylum. He shall be taken to said aslyum
immediately, the safety of said lunatic and
others requiring it. It is hereby certified
upon the proof as part of this order that the
date of the first attack of lunacy was about
six weeks or two months ago."

Middaugh, Lucy:
37/120 - July 17, 1893.
    "An inquest upon Lucy Middaugh, an idiot,
was this day held and recorded."

39/383 - November 11, 1901.
    "It appearing to the satisfaction of the
court that Mary Wheeler and John Wood, lunatics,
and Amos Carr, Cynthia Ann Burton, Minta
Traylor, John Traylor, Lucy Middaugh, Did
Nicholls, Isaiah Stepter, Minnie McGinnis,
and Mary Griffith, idiots, are still alive,
in the care of their committees, and have not
estate sufficient for their support, and that
their parents are still unable to support them."

Morgan, _____ :
29/251 - March 19, 1874.
    "It appearing to the court that _____
Morgan, a pauper lunatic, was confined in the
jail of Greenup County in the custody and control of Charles Callihan, Jailer of Greenup
County as a committee, and had not sufficient
estate for his support and no friends or parents
able to support him, and that said pauper lunatic was taken care of by said Jailer Callihan
from the 20th day of May 1873 to the 22nd day
of June 1873, making 34 days.
    It is therefore ordered that the allowance
at the rate of $200.00 per annum be paid said
Callihan for the proportionable time he kept
said pauper lunatic, which amounts to the sum

of $18.62 and that same be certified to the
Auditor for payment under the act approved
March 28, 1872."

Morton, David:
L/151 - October 7, 1837.
   "On motion of the attorney for the Commonwealth, it is ordered that a jury be summoned
to ascertain whether David Morton be or be
not of sound mind, and said David Morton being
personally present, and thereupon came a jury
towit: Charlton Shepherd, James Gilkerson,
Benjamin S. Rankins, Thomas H. Poage, John
D. Williams, Henry Hays, John H. Chinn, James
M. Cartney, Pleasant Ellington, Nathaniel Davis,
Russell A. Dayton and John M. Hart, who being
elected, tried and sworn well and truly to
inquire whether David Morton be or be not of
sound mind, and if he be of unsound mind,
whether he was so at the time of his birth
or became so afterwards, and thereupon the
court appointed William R. Beatty, Esq., to
attend to the inquisition on behalf of said
David Morton, and the evidence being heard,
the jury upon their oaths returned the following verdit, towit: 'We, the jury, find David
Morton to be a man of very weak mind and incompetent to the discharge of business, though
we do not think him either an idiot or a
lunatic, and that he has an estate of five
or six hundred dollars.'"

Murphy, John:
35/38 - February 26, 1885 (age 26).
   "This day the attorney for the Commonwealth
filed an information as follows, towit: To
Hon. H. E. Cole, Judge of the Greenup Circuit
Court, I am reliably informed that John Murphy
is a person of unsound mind and an idiot, and
therefore ask that a jury be impanneled (sic)
to pass upon the subject. (signed) B. E.
Roe, Commonwealth Attorney perotem (sic).
   Ordered by the Court that B. F. Bennett,
Esq., an attorney of this court, be and he
is hereby appointed to defend for and on behalf
of the person under trial. To inquire comes
a jury, towit: Don Hendershot, James McCoy,
John Lewis, David Bush, F. B. Meadows, James

Brown, H. S. Curry, Jack Gammon, James Pugh,
Jacob Rake, William Posten, and W. P. Bennett,
who being duly elected and sworn according
to law, after hearing the evidence returned
the following verdict: 'We, the jury, find
from the evidence that John Murphy is a person
of unsound mind and an idiot; that the unsoundness of mind has existed from birth; that he
was born in Greenup County and resides in
Greenup County, and is 26 years old; that he
was not brought into this state for the purpose
of becoming a charge upon the Commonwealth;
that he owns no estate of any kind; that his
father is living and mother is dead; and
(Father) resides in Ohio, and he has not estate
sufficient to support the person under trial;
and said Murphy is not capable of laboring
in whole or in part for his support.' (signed)
W. P. Bennett, foreman.
    It is therefore ordered that William Murphy
be appointed a committee to take charge of
said John Murphy and provide him with suitable
diet, clothing, etc., and that he be allowed
therefor at the rate of $75.00 per annum from
this date, to be paid upon the further order
of this court. It is ordered that said William
Murphy give bond and security for the faithful
performance of his duty in this case."

35/75 - March 2, 1885.
    "Ordered that B. F. Brown be appointed com-
mittee of John Murphy instead of William Murphy.
Whereupon said Brown appeared and with B. F.
Ferguson as surety, who is approved, executed
bond as required by law."

36/291 - March 1, 1890 (age 32).
    "This day the attorney for the Commonwealth
filed an information as follows, towit:
    To Hon. A. E. Cole, Judge of the Greenup
Circuit Court: I am reliably informed that
John Murphy, is a person of unsound mind and
a _____ and therefore ask that a jury be
impaneled to pass upon the subject. (signed)
James H. Sallee, Commonwealth Attorney, 14th
Judicial District.
    Ordered by the court that D. J. McCoy, Esq.,
an attorney of this court, be and he is hereby

appointed to defend for and on behalf of the
person under trial. To inquire comes a jury,
towit: J. E. Pollock, L. H. Carnegy, I. N.
Dysard, John Blankenship, G. W. McLane, James
Ruggles, J. H. W. Thomson, J. H. Chinn, Thomas
Tynes, Charles Pierce, John Allen and John
Nicholls, who were duly sworn according to
law, and after hearing the evidence, and the
said John Murphy being present in court,
returned the following verdict: 'We of the
jury find from the evidence that John Murphy
is a person of unsound mind and an idiot; that
the unsoundness of mind has existed from his
birth; that he was born in Greenup County,
Kentucky, and resides in same, and is about
32 years old; that he was not brought into
this state for the purpose of becoming a charge
upon the Commonwealth; that he owns no estate
of any kind; that his father is dead and mother
dead, and left no estate sufficient to support
the person under trial; and said John Murphy
is not capable of laboring in whole or in part
for his support; and has heretofore been
adjudged an idiot.' (signed) Thomas E. Tynes,
foreman.
     It is therefore ordered that J. Watt Womack
be appointed a committee to take charge of
said John Murphy and provide him with suitable
diet, clothing, etc., and that he be allowed
therefor at the rate of $75.00 per annum from
this date, to be paid upon further orders of
this Court. The said J. Watt Womack with J.
T. Womack as his surety, who is accepted and
approved by the Court, executed bond to the
Commonwealth of Kentucky as committee aforesaid,
conditioned according to law."

39/368 - November 7, 1901.
     "It appearing to the satisfaction of the
Court that Gracie Guilkey, Hannah Davis, Ella
Jennings, Birdie Traylor, William C. Kitts,
James A. Kitts, Bennie Adkins, John Murphy,
and Martha Wadkins, idiots, are still alive,
in the care of their committees and have not
sufficient estate for their support, and that
their parents are still unable to support them,
it is ordered that the allowance of $75.00
per annum each for their support be continued

from the last payment, and that the same be
copied and certified to the Auditor of Public
Accounts for payment."

Neville, William:
G/382 - October 4, 1827 (age 9).
   "On motion of the attorney for the Commonwealth it is ordered that a jury be empannelled
(sic) to inquire into the state of mind of
William Neville, son of Ann Neville, and to
ascertain whether the said William Neville
hath any estate either by descent or purchase
or in any other wise, and thereupon came a
jury, towit: John Stewart, Robert Thompson,
Frederick Burger, Daniel Blankinship, James
Gilkerson, Joseph Kelly, William Mayhew, John
Cracraft, Abraham Meadows, Aaron Bush, Alexander
Rankins and Daniel Perry who being sworn to
inquire into the facts aforesaid returned the
following report, towit: 'We, the jury, find
that William Neville is about 9 years of age,
is a person of unsound mind and an idiot, and
that he has no estate whatsoever and that his
mother, who is a widow, is extremely poor,'
   And thereupon it is ordered that his said
mother, Ann Neville, be appointed a committee
to keep, take care of and maintain the said
William Neville."

I/237 - April 12, 1834.
   "Ordered that it be certified to the Auditor
of Public Accounts that William Neville, an
idiot, of whom Ann Neville was by order of
the court appointed a committee, departed this
life about one month after the 10th of October
last. That said committee be allowed the sum
of $5.00 for keeping said idiot until his death
and $10.00 for the funeral expenses of said
idiot at his death. The court considering
that sum to be such for the same."

Nicholls, Did:
34/121 - August 27, 1883 (age 16).
   "Upon the motion of the attorney for the
Commonwealth it is ordered that a writ of de
idota inquirendo issue in the case of Did
Nicholls, an idiot, returnable immediately,
to inquire into the state of mind of said Did

Nicholls, and it is ordered that George E.
Roe, Esq., be appointed counsel for said Did
Nicholls. Whereupon came a jury, towit:
Matthew Warnock. Reasen Virgin, James King,
H. W. Peters, H. C. Mackoy, A. B. Martin, Mason
Burns, James Dugan, Thomas Chinn, Taylor
Warnock, Henry Deidrick and D. B. Davissen,
who being sworn according to law returned the
following verdict: 'We, the jury, impaneled
and sworn to inquire into the condition of
mind of Did Nicholls, and having heard the
evidence and a view of said Did Nicholls in
open court, do find that the said Did Nicholls
is an idiot, destitute of mind since her birth;
that she is 16 years of age and was born in
Greenup County, Kentucky; and that she has
no estate either in possession, reversion or
remainder; that her parents are both living
and reside in this County; that they have no
estate sufficient to support the said idiot;
that she is not capable of laboring in whole
or in part for her support; and that she was
not brought into this state and county for
the purpose of becoming a charge upon the
Commonwealth.' Given under our hands this
27 day of August 1882. (signed) A. B. Martin,
one of the Jury.
    And it is therefore ordered that John Syden-
stricker be appointed her committee to take
charge of said Did Nicholls and provide her
with suitable diet, clothing, etc. and that
he be allowed therefor at the rate of $75.00
per annum from this date, to be paid upon the
further order of the court."

34/167 - September 6, 1883.
    "The committee, John Sydenstriker, failing
to give bond and declining to continue as such,
it is now ordered that B. F. Brown be appointed
committee for said idiot. He thereupon appeared
in court and with R. A. Callihan as his surety,
who is accepted and approved by the Court,
executed bond, conditioned according to law."

39/383 - November 11, 1901.
    "It appearing to the satisfaction of the
court that Mary Wheeler and John Wood, lunatics,
and Amos Carr, Cynthia Ann Burton, Minta
Traylor, John Traylor, Lucy Middaugh, Did

Nicholls, Isaiah Stepter, Minnie McGinnis,
and Mary Griffith, idiots, are still alive,
in the care of their committees, and have not
estate sufficient for their support, and that
their parents are still unable to support them."

Prichett, Nancy:
U/494 - May 17, 1860 (age 9).
   "On the motion of the attorney for the Commonwealth, it is ordered that an inquest be held
by a jury to ascertain whether Nancy Prichett
is of unsound mind, and thereupon the court
appointed S. K. Handerson, a member of this
bar, to represent and protect the interest
and rights of the said Nancy Prichett, and
said Nancy Prichett was brought into open court,
a jury was then empannelled (sic) and sworn,
towit: Wm. Hampton, John Alley, Robt Clutz,
Clem Swearingen, John Barney, Jeff Loper, L.
Rife, Samuel Powell, Chas. Callahan, Jno L.
Gray, Elisha Ferguson and Jno. I. Stewart.
   The said Nancy Prichett being in court and
personally in the presence of the jury, and
the jury having heard the evidence, upon their
oaths returned the following verdict, towit:
   'We, the jury, find from the evidence that
Nancy Prichett, the person whom we have under
charge, is of unsound mind, and we find that
it is a lunatic; that is it has, as far as
we can learn, lost its mind by reason of a
burn on the inside of the thigh and the conse-
quences following thereafter; she was so burned
when about one year old very severely and it
dident (sic) heal up for about two years, and
when it did heal up its loss of mind began
manifesting itself either caused by or attending fits which then commenced on it and have
since continued. While it is subject to fits,
we consider it as deranged in mind, when the
fits are not affecting it, or on it; she was
born in this county and about 9 years old,
resides here and was not brought into the state
for the purpose of being made a charge to the
Commonwealth. She has no estate either in
her possession, reversion or remainder. Her
father is dead, her mother is alive and resides
in this county and has no estate sufficient
to support the said child, and the said Nancy

Prichett is incapable of laboring in whole
or in part for her support.' (signed) Wm
Hampton.
The court being satisfied with the inquest,
it is adjudged that the said Nancy Prichett
is a lunatic and that the other facts found
by the jury are true."

W/337 - November 21, 1863 (11 or 12 years old).
"We, the jury, find that Nancy Pritchard
is a lunatic; that she lost her mind since
her birthday, viz: when about 2 years old.
She was born in Greenup County, Kentucky, and
has ever since and still resides in said county;
is 11 or 12 years old, and that she has no
estate, either in possession, reversion or
remainder; that her mother only is alive and
resides in Greenup County, Kentucky, and has
not estate sufficient to support her; that
she is not capable of laboring in whole or
in part for her support. (signed) J. L. Collins,
foreman.
And the Court being satisfied with the
inquest, it is adjudged by the court that the
said Nancy Pritchet is a lunatic and that the
other facts found by the jury in the verdict
are true."

Raison, Lewis M. M.:
D/264 - July 31, 1818.
"On motion of the attorney for the Common-
wealth, it is ordered that a Writ of Deidioto
Inquirendo issues to the Sheriff, returnable
today, to inquire by and have inquest whether
Lewis Raison be of unsound mind and make such
other inquests as required by law."

D/273 - July 31, 1818 (age 32).
"The Writ of Deidioto Inquirendo issued and
returnable on this day to make inquisition
whether Lewis Raison is of unsound mind, etc.,
was returned by the Sheriff together with the
inquisition taken thereon, which inquisition
and Sheriff's return on said Writ are in the
words and figures as follows, to-wit: 'In
obedience to the Commonwealth of the within
Writ, I have on this day summoned and caused
to come before me at the house of Lewis Raison

in Greenupsburg, Jury of 12 good lawful men of Greenup County who, after being duly sworn and charged by me and after hearing sundry witnesses examined before them, on oath returned their inquirition signed and sealed by the said jurors, which I herewith return enclosed.' Given under my hand this 31st day of July 1818. (signed) Will Ward, D.S. (Deputy Sheriff) for Francis Waring, Sheriff.

An inquisition taken for the Commonwealth before William Ward, Deputy Sheriff of Greenup by the oaths of Abram Ward, John Rice, Amos Chitwood, Wyncoox Warner, John Githun, Daniel Blankenship, John Howe, John Culver, Thomson Ward, Thomas Ruhcards, Francis Gaines, and James Ward on the 31st day of July 1818 at the house of Lewis Raison in pursuance of a Writ deidiota inquirendo to the said Sheriff directed the said jurors, being first duly sworn by the said William Ward, Deputy Sheriff as aforesaid, and charged according to law, to make inquest and find upon the evidence produced and examined before them that the said Lewis Raison in the said Writ mentioned is of unsound mind, that he has labored under a considerable degree of mental derangement for about three weeks. We find his insanity has been occasioned by misfortune and that he was not born an idiot. We cannot find what probability there is of his recovering the proper use of his intellectual powers as he has heretofore possessed and enjoyed them. We also find that the said Lewis Raison is about 32 years of age and he resides with his family in Greenupsburg, he being a married man and having a wife and four children. We also find that the said Lewis Raison owns and is possessed of a house and lot in Greenupsburg of the value of $400, one negro woman and child of the value of $600, four beds and furniture of the value of $200, one roan mare of the value of $30, household and kitchen furniture of the value of $200, debts by notes and amounts to the amount as we suppose of $200, 2 cows and one calf of the value of $30, one watch of the value of $15, 15 head of sheep of the value of $30, and one rifle gun of the value of $8, amounting in whole to the sum of $1,712.

Given under our hands and seals this 31st day
of July 1818.
And the Court, not now being sufficiently
advised who are proper persons to approve as
a committee to take charge of the said Lewis
Riason, took time. "

D/287 - August 1, 1818.
"Ordered that John M. McConnell and Henry
Green be appointed a committee to take charge
of Lewis Raisin and his property and deal with
the same as the law directs, which said Lewis
having been found to be of unsound mind by
an inquirention returned and recorded on the
5th day of this term held in pursuance of a
Writ of deidioto inquirendo issued agreeable
to an order of this court."

Eo/343 - November 1, 1819.
"Ordered that John Young and John Powell
the committee appointed over Lewis M. Raison
and his effects, found insane by an inquisition
taken under a writ of deideoto inquirendo,
be ruled to report to this court by tomorrow
morning the present state of his mind and also
as the situation of his property."

Eo/364 - November 4, 1819.
"On motion of Lewis M. Reason (sic), and
upon evidence produced and heard and the report
of his committee being filed, it seems to the
Court that the senses of the said Lewis M.
Raison are restored, it is therefore ordered
that he be discharged from his committee and
his property restored."

F/273 - October 15, 1822.
"On motion of the attorney for the Commonwealth, it is ordered that a Writ of Deidioto
Inquirendo issue to the Sheriff of Greenup
County returnable on Friday next, commanding
him to impanel a jury to inquire and make
inquest whether Lewis M. M. Raison be of unsound
mind or not, and make such other inquest as
required by law and make report according to
law."

F/280 - October 15, 1822 (age 37).

"The Writ of Deidioto Inquirendo issued and
returned on Friday next to make inquirition
whether Lewis M. M. Raison is of unsound mind
was this day returned by the Sheriff together
with the report of the jury thereon, which
report and return of the Sheriff are ordered
to be recorded and are as follows, to-wit:
'Executed 15th October 1822 and the report
of the jury herewith returned.' (signed) G.
Davis, D.S. (Deputy Sheriff) for B. Chinn,
Sheriff Greenup County.
    'We, the jury, do report, being first duly
sworn, that Lewis M. M. Raison is of unsound
mind and that he has been so from about the
1st day of August last and that he hath not
been so from his birth, and that he has lost
the same by casualty, and no probability of
his recovering his senses, and is about the
age of 36, and resides in the Jail of Greenup
County at this time and at other times rambling
from place to place, the amount of property
is one house and lot in Greenupsburg, 1 negro
woman, 3 children, 1 mare, 6 head of cattle,
3 beds and furniture and household furnitures
amount to best proof as can obtain to $1,000.00.
Given under our hands this 15th day of October
1822. (signed) Edward Eastham, John Morton,
John Pratt, John McAlister, John Peebles, James
VanBibber, James Chriswith, Thomas Richards,
Nicholas Nicholes, Thomas Sammons, John C.
Thomas, Jacob Kouns.
    And thereupon it is ordered that Smith King
be appointed a committee to take into his charge
and safe keeping the said Lewis M. Raison,
and it is ordered to be certified to the Auditor
of Public Accounts that Smith King is entitled
to $50.00 for the safe keeping of Lewis M.
Raison, a lunatic, until the next April term
of this court."

F/334 - April 14, 1823.
    "It appearing to the satisfaction of the
Court that Lewis M. M. Raison, a lunatic, (found
so by a jury duly impanelled and sworn according to law for that purpose) has recovered
his senses. It is therefore, on Motion of
the said Lewis M. M. Raison, ordered that he
be discharged from his committee appointed

at the last October term of this court, and
that the control of his estate be vested in
him as heretofore, and it is ordered that it
be certified to the Auditor of Public Accounts
that Smith King, the committee of the said
Lewis M. M. Raison, be allowed the sum of $50.00
for supporting and taking care of the said
Lewis M. M. Raison for the last six months,
satisfactory proof being made to the court
that the said Smith King has supported and
taken care of the said Lewis M. M. Raison agree-
ably to the order of the court made at the
October term last."

G/242 - July 3, 1826.
"On motion of the attorney for the Commonwealth, it is ordered that the Sheriff summon
a jury to come here immediately to inquire
into the sanity or insanity of Lewis M. Raison,
and thereupon came a jury, towit: William
Dupuy, Robinson M. Biggs, Alexander Rankin,
William Biggs, John Morton, Aaron Tuffs, Lewis
Thomas, John VanBibber, Clement H. Waring,
Benjamin S. Rankins, James McGuire and Benjamin
Powell, who being elected, tried and sworn
well and truly to inquire into the sanity or
insanity of said Lewis M. Raison, returned
the following verdict, towit: 'We, the jury,
find that the said Lewis M. Raison is of unsound
mind and a lunatic and that he has not estate
more than sufficient to support his wife and
children.'
    And thereupon it is ordered that Benjamin
Powell is appointed a committee to take care
of said Lewis M. Raison and convey him to the
lunatic hospital at Lexington."

I/352 - October 11, 1834.
"On motion of the attorney for the Commonwealth, it is ordered that John Young be
appointed a committee to take charge of the
estate of Lewis M. Raison, who was found to
be a lunatic at a former term of this court,
upon his entering into bond in the Clerk's
Office in the penalty of $1,000.00, conditioned
for the faithful appropriation of the money
that may come into his hands and the performance
of his duties as committee."

NOTE: K/401 - July 6, 1837: states Lewis
M. M. Raison and Aramatha K. Raison, both
deceased, have 10 heirs and are possessed of
five negros at the time of their deaths: Tenar,
George, Lydia, Jacob and Mariah.
M/80 - October 12, 1839: sets out 8 of
the ten heirs of Lewis M. M. Raison and Aramatha
K. Raison as being: Eveline, Lewis (N.),
Charles (Louis), Molly Ann C., Emily (M. M.),
Julia Ann and Louisa, as well as three son-
in-laws: William (Fletcher) Mavity, Daniel
Higgins, and Benjamin Ulen, whom I have learned
from other sources were married to Marie
Antoinette Raison Mavity, Sophia M. T. Raison
Higgins, and Betsy (Elizabeth) Y. Raison Ulen,
daughters of Lewis and Aramatha K. Raison.
These two entries are in reference to a law-
suit resulting from John Young (father of
Aramatha K. Raison) holding and not releasing
to the estate for sale at public auction the
negro slaves, Tenar, a woman, and George, a
child.

Ramey, Josiah:
36/472 - February 23, 1892.
"An inquest was this day held upon Josiah
Ramey, a lunatic, and duly recorded."

37/55 - September 7, 1892.
"Upon proof being made to the satisfaction
of the Court that Josiah Ramey, heretofore
found to be a lunatic, is still alive, in the
care of G. C. Riffe, his committee, and has
not sufficient estate for his support, and
that his parents are still unable to support
him, it is ordered by the Court that G. C.
Riffe, his committee, be allowed at the rate
of $75.00 per annum for his support from the
finding of the jury at a former term of this
court to this date, which is ordered to be
certified to the Auditor of Public Accounts
for payment."

Rankins, John B.:
W/276 - May 23, 1863 (age 32).
"George M. Thomas attorney, for the Common-
wealth, being absent, it is ordered that William
C. Ireland be appointed attorney for the Common-

wealth protem, and on his motion it is ordered
at a writ of de idota inquirendo issue in the
case of John B. Rankins to inquire into the
state of mind of the said John B. Rankins,
and it is ordered that George E. Roe, Esq.,
be appointed counsel for said John B. Rankins,
and the said John B. Rankins being personally
in the presence of the jury, whereupon came
a jury towit: Saml B. Hornbuckle, Isaac N.
Dysert, John Nicholls, Jas. M. Brammer, Hiram
Kiser, Jesse Davidson, Ignatius Miller, N.
F. Thom, James Sutherland, Lexius Riffe, Danl
Callahan, and David Bryson, who being sworn
according to law returned the following verdict,
towit: 'We, the jury, find that John B. Rankins
is a lunatic, that he lost his mind about 5
years ago, dont (sic) know the cause of the
loss of his mind. He was born in Greenup
County, Ky., has always heretofore and now
resides in said county. He has no estate of
his own either in possession, reversion or
remainder. His father only is alive, and able
to support him, who now resides in Greenup
County. He is not able to labor in whole or
in part for his support, and is 32 years old.'
(signed) L. Riffe, foreman.
    And the Court being satisfied with the
inquest, it is adjudged by the Court that the
said John B. Rankins is a lunatic, and that
the other facts found by the jury in their
verdict are true."

Ratcliff, Jerimah:
16/141 - February 16, 1875.
    "It appearing to the satisfaction of the
Court that Jerimah Ratcliff is an imbecile
and unfit to take charge and proper care of
his estate, it is ordered that Eli Cooper be
appointed his committee."

Ray, William:
T/102 - November 19, 1857 (age 3).
    "On the motion of the attorney for the Common-
wealth, who represents that he has been informed
that William Ray of this County is a person
of unsound mind, it is ordered that a Writ
of De Idiota Inquirendo issue, returnable
immediately, to inquire into the state of the

mind of said William Ray, and whether he has
any estate etc., and it is ordered that William
C. Ireland be appointed counsel for the said
William Ray. Whereupon the said William Ray
was brought into Court, Archer Womack, John
N. Bates, Aaron Bush, James J. Harvey, Henry
Hays, Jesse Davisson, Jacob Howe, O. F. McKoy,
Benjamin King, John W. H. Warnock, Wm. Bryson,
and Jno P. Jones were impannelled (sic), sworn
and charged according to law as a jury of
inquest under the said wit, and having heard
evidence returned, the following verdict, viz:
'We, the jury, find that William Ray is an
idiot; that he is about 3 years old; that he
was born in Carter County, Kentucky, where
his parents now reside; that the said William
Ray has resided with Edward Martin in Greenup
County about two years past, and he has no
estate either in possession, reversion or
remainder; that his parents are alive and have
not estate sufficient to support the said
William Ray; that the said William Ray is
incapable of laboring in whole or in part for
his support. We further find that the said
idiot has not been brought into this county
for the purpose of receiving a support out
of the Treasury.'
    Wherefore it is adjudged by the Court that
the said William Ray is an idiot, and Edward
Martin is appointed a committee to take charge
of said William Ray, and provide for him suitable lodging etc, and that he be allowed therefor at the rate of $50.00 per annum from this
date, to be paid out of the treasury of this
state upon the further order of this court."

T/416 - July 19, 1858.
    "It appearing to the satisfaction of the
court that William Ray, who was found to be
an idiot at a former term of this court, is
still alive, in the care of his committee,
that no change has taken place in his mind,
physical condition or estate since the original
inquest. Wherefore it is ordered that the
allowance of $50.00 per annum be continued
from the last allowance which is ordered to
be certified to the Auditor for payment."

Ringgold, Phoebe:
29/253 - March 19, 1874.
   "It appearing to the satisfaction of the
court that Phoebe Ringold, a pauper lunatic,
of Greenup County was in the custody and control
of James Roberts, as her committee, and has
no estate sufficient for her support and no
friends or parents able to support her, and
that the pauper lunatic was taken care of by
said Roberts from the 3rd day of June 1873
until the 10th day of September 1873 (both
days inclusive), making 100 days.
   It is therefore ordered that the allowance
at the rate of $200.00 per annum be paid to
the said James Roberts for the porportionable
time he kept the said pauper lunatic, which
amounts to the sum of $54.79, and that the
same be certified to the Auditor for payment
under the Act approved March 28, 1872."

Sexton, Emily:
V/376 - May 14, 1862 (age 8).
   "On motion of the attorney for the Commonwealth, who represents that he has been informed
that Emily Sexton of this County is a person
of unsound mind, it is ordered that a writ
of de idiota inquirendo issued, returnable
immediately, to inquire into the state of mind
of the said Sexton, whether they had any estate
etc., and it is ordered that L. W. Andrews
be appointed counsel for said Sexton. Whereupon the said Sexton was brought into open
court and Wm. P. Bennett, James Bryan, J. P.
Winter, Jno R. Barney, A. Thompson, Jas. Downs,
Arent B. Bush, Jesse Alexander, Frank Waring,
J. M. Craycraft, Wm. H. Warnock, and D. J.
McKoy were impannelled (sic) and sworn to try
said case as a jury of inquest under said writ,
and having heard the evidence, returned the
following verdict, towit: 'We, the jury,
impanelled, sworn to inquire of the state of
mind of said Sexton do say that she is in her
8th year and that she is not an idiot or a
lunatic, but that she is a feeble minded child
and has been so, as far as we are able to
assertain from the testimony, from her birth,
and is from a deficiency in her vocal organs
unable to speak or articulate. She was born
in Greenup County. Her Father is dead, but

her Mother is living and resides in Greenup
County and has no estate sufficient for the
support of said child. The said child has
no estate in possession, reversion or remainder
and is incapable of laboring in whole or in
part for her support. We deem her a fit subject
to be sent to the institution and recommend
that she be admitted into that institution.'
(signed) James Bryan, one of the jury."

Shipton, George:
P/181 - April 25, 1849 (age 27).
   "On motion of the attorney for the Commonwealth, who represents that George Shipton
is a person of unsound mind, it is ordered
that a writ de lunatico inquirendo issue for
the purpose of inquiring into the state of
the mind of the said George Shipton and whether
he has any estate, and if any, the nature and
extent thereof, and William L. Poage, Esq.,
is appointed counsel for the said George
Shipton. Whereupon the said writ having issued
and being returned executed, the jury summoned,
Hugh A. Poage, L. W. Andrews, George Tanner,
John Anglin, John C. Fugud, Richard Scott,
William Hite, J. H. Senate, William Hampton,
William Dupuy, James E. Nichols, and William
Biggs, who were sworn and charged to inquire,
etc., and having heard the evidence, returned
the following verdict. towit:
   'We, the jury, find that George Shipton is
a lunatic, is 27 years of age, a resident of
Greenup County where he was born, has no estate
for his support, his general health until about
11 years age was good, when he became diseased
with white swelling and afflicted with fits
which have become more frequent, none of his
relations insane, is of temperate habits, temper
formerly good but now unstable, affectionate
to his relatives, tolerable English education
and has no family.'
   It is therefore considered by the Court
that the said George Shipton is a lunatic and
that he be taken to and confined in the Lunatic
Asylum at Lexington, there to remain until
discharged therefrom, and that Mary Shipton,
his mother, be and she is hereby appointed
to take charge of the said George Shipton and

convey him to said asylum and deliver him to
the officers of the same, and it is further
ordered that James Rouse assist the said Mary
Shipton in conveying said George Shipton to
said asylum, and it is further ordered that
the said Mary Shipton and James Rouse be and
they are hereby allowed the sum of $10.00 each
for their services in going to and returning
from said asylum, all which is ordered to be
certified."

Smiley, Josephine:
N/452 - April 4, 1844.
  "On motion of the attorney for the Commonwealth, it is ordered that the Sheriff of
Greenup County summon twelve housekeepers to
appear here immediately to inquire whether
Josephine Smiley, who is now in open court,
be or be not of sound mind, and if she be of
unsound mind, whether she was so at the time
of her birth or became so afterwards, and of
the property she has, and thereupon came a
jury towit: Jonsa D. Glover, John Culver,
Moses McKoy, Andrew I. Sellards, William S.
Guiger, Nathaniel S. Warner, Samuel G. Glover,
Thomas Howell, E. J. Hockaday, Wm. Craycraft,
John T. Lawson and Hezekiah Morton, who being
elected, tried and sworn well and truly to
inquire into and ascertain the facts for which
they were summoned to inquire upon their oath
returned the following verdict, to-wit: 'That
the said Josephine Smiley is an idiot and that
has been so since her birth, and that she hath
no estate whatsoever of her own, her father
and mother are both alive and in good health.
That her father has about 200 acres of land
worth $3.00 per acre, two horses and some cattle
and hogs.'
  The said Josephine Smiley being in open
court, witnesses being examined and counsel
appeared.
  It is therefore ordered that it be certified
that Walter Smiley is appointed committee to
take care of said Josephine Smiley."

Smith, Jennie Belle:
37/355 - April 3, 1895.

"An inquest was this day held upon Jennie
Belle Smith, a lunatic, and recorded."

39/379 - November 8, 1901.
"It appearing to the satisfaction of the
court that Jennie Belle Smith, a lunatic, is
still alive, in the care of her committee and
has not estate sufficient for her support,
and that her parents are still unable to support
her, it is ordered that the allowance of $75.00
per annum for her support be continued from
the last payment and that the same be copied
and certified to the Auditor of Public Accounts
for payment."

Smith, John:
37/302 - November 8, 1894.
"Inquests were this day held upon Mary
Wheeler, a lunatic, and John Smith, an idiot,
and each duly recorded."

37/498 - April 8, 1896.
"It appearing to the satisfaction of the
Court that John Smith, an idiot, was alive
in the 20th day of January 1896, and had not
sufficient estate for his support, and that
his parents were unable to support him, it
is ordered that the allowance of $75.00 per
annum for his support be continued from the
last payment up to and including the 20th day
of January, 1896, that being the date of said
idiot's death, and that the same be certified
to the Auditor for payment."

Steenrod, Jacob: (brother of James Steenrod)
R/328 - May 31, 1855 (age 16).
"On motion of the attorney for the Commonwealth, who represents that he has been informed
that James Steenrod and Jacob Steenrod of this
county are persons of unsound mind, it is
ordered that a Writ of de-inquirendo de Idiota
issue, returnable immediately, to inquire into
the state of the mind of the said James Steenrod
and Jacob Steenrod and whether they have any
estate, etc., and it is ordered that Thomas
F. Hazelrigg, Esq., be appointed counsel for
the said James Steenrod and Jacob Steenrod,
whereupon the said James and Jacob Steenrod

were brought into open court and Nicholas
Savage, Richard Jones, Jesse Poynter, John
C. Burk, Jesse Davidson William Craycraft,
Carlisle Hunt, Joseph B. Davidson, George
Tanner, Thomas I. Poteet, Edward Brooks, and
Alexander Davis were impannelled (sic) sworn
and charged according to law as a jury of
inquest under said Writ, and having heard the
evidence returned the following verdict: 'We,
the jury, find that James Steenrod and Jacob
Steenrod are persons of unsound mind and idiots;
that they were destitute of mind from infancy;
they were born in and reside in Greenup County
and were not brought to this state for the
purpose of becoming a charge upon the Commonwealth; that their father has been dead about
10 years and was subject to fits, and that
their mother is still living in Greenup County,
and that she has not sufficient estate to
support the said James Steenrod and Jacob
Steenrod; that they are incapable of laboring
in whole or in part for their support. We
further find that James Steenrod has before
been found an idiot, and that no change has
taken place in his mind since the original
inquest, and that Jacob Steenrod has never
been found an idiot. We also find that said
James Steenrod is about 22 years of age and
that said Jacob Steenrod is about 16 years
of age.' (signed) Nicholas Savage, Richard
Jones, Jesse Poynter, John C. Burk, Jesse
Davidson, William Craycraft, Carlisle Hunt,
Joseph B. Davidson, George Tanner, Thomas L.
Poteet, Edward Brooks, Alexander Davis.
    It is therefore ordered that Elizabeth
Steenrod be appointed a committee to take charge
of said James Steenrod and Jacob Steenrod and
provide for them suitable diet, clothing, etc.,
and that she be allowed at the rate of $50.00
per annum from the last allowance for the
support of James Steenrod, which is ordered
to be certified to the Auditor for payment,
and she is allowed at the rate of $50.00 per
annum from this date to be paid out of the
treasury of this state upon further order of
this court."

S/216 - November 15, 1856.

"Elizabeth Steenrod, committee for James Steenrod and Jacob Steenrod, idiots of this county, having departed this life since the last term of this court, it is ordered that Benj. F. King be appointed a committee for said idiots, and proof being adduced that said idiots are in all respects in the same condition as in which they were at the last allowance made to them by this court, it is ordered the allowance be continued to each of said idiots and paid to Benj. F. King, their committee, which is ordered to be certified to the Auditor of Public Accounts for payment."

U/569 - May 23, 1860 (age 21).
"We, the jury, say that James Steenrod and Jacob Steenrod, whom we have in charge, are of unsound mind, that they are idiots. That they have been destitute of mind from their birth. Jacob was born in Greenup County, Kentucky, and is about 21 years old; James was born in Mason County, Kentucky, and is about 33 years old or near that, and they have not been brought into this state for the purpose of becoming a charge upon it, they have each an undivided interest of 1/6th in about 24 or 25 acres of 2nd or 3rd rate land in this county worth about a dollar a year rent per acre, and they have no other estate in possession, reversion or remainder. Their parents are dead, and the said James and Jacob are incapable of laboring in whole or in part for their support. They have before been found by the verdict of a jury and Judgment in this court idiots, and no change has since taken place in their minds, physical condition or estate since the former inquest. (signed) John T. Lawson.
It is therefore adjudged by the Court that James and Jacob Steenrod are idiots and Benjamin F. King, their former committee, having tendered his resignation in writing. It is ordered that Moses F. Dupuy be appointed to take charge of said James and Jacob Steenrod, and provide for them suitable diet, clothing, etc., and that the allowance of $50.00 per annum each be continued from the last payment, which is ordered to be certified to the Auditor.

It is further ordered that said Moses F.
Dupuy gave bond and security, for the faithful
performance of his duties in the penalty of
$200.00. Whereupon he, together with George
E. Roe as his security, executed bond accord-
ingly, which is approved by the court."

X/458 - September 5, 1865 (age 24).
   "We, the jury, find that Jacob Steenrod,
the person under charge, is an idiot, that
he is destitute of mind from infancy. He was
born in Greenup County, Kentucky, and has always
lived in the state and is 24 years of age.
He is the owner of 1/6 of 24 acres of land
in Greenup County, which 24 acres of land is
worth $60.00 per year rent. His parents are
dead. He is not capable of laboring in whole
or in part for his support. He was found to
be an idiot by a former inquest in this court.
(signed) Lewis Nichols, foreman.
   And the court being satisfied with the
inquest adjudges that the said Jacob Steenrod
is an idiot and has not sufficient estate for
his support and his parents are unable to
support him. It is therefore ordered that
the sum of $50.00 per annum be allowed for
his support and maintenance from the last allowance, payable to James Bryan, his committee."

26/144 - September 7, 1870 (age 31).
   "We, the jury, find that Jacob Steenrod,
whom we have in charge, is an idiot and has
been destitute of mind from infancy; that his
father and mother are both dead; that he was
born in Kentucky and has lived here ever since;
that he is 31 years of age, and he has not
estate in possession, reversion or remainder,
except that he owns one moiety of 3 acres of
3rd rate land in Greenup County which descended
from his father to himself and brother, and
which is not sufficient for his support, and
he is incapable of laboring for his own support
either in part or in whole, and that he has
heretofore been found an idiot by a verdict
of a jury and Judgment of this court. (Signed)
H. C. Mackoy, foreman.
   It is, therefore, ordered that John Stepter
be continued as committee to take charge of

said Jacob Steenrod and provide him with suitable diet, clothing, etc. and that he be allowed
therefor at the rate of $50.00 per annum from
the last payment, to be paid upon the further
orders of this court, which is ordered to be
certified to the Auditor."

31/23 - September 6, 1875.
  "We, the jury, find from the evidence that
the defendant, Jacob Steenrod is an idiot;
that he was born in Greenup County about 1837
and has always lived in said County; that he
has no estate in possession or reversion or
remainder except about 4 1/4 acres of land
in Greenup County worth $12.00 an acre; that
his parents are dead and left no estate except
the above named, and that he is not capable
of laboring to any extent for his support,
and he has heretofore been found an idiot,
and that said land is not of any value to him
above the expense of keeping upon expenses
on same. (signed) Geo. W. Callihan.
  It is therefore ordered that John Stepter
be appointed a committee to take charge of
said Jacob Steenrod and provide him with suitable diet, clothing, etc. and that he be allowed
therefor at the rate of $75.00 per annum from
this date. It is further ordered that said
Stepter execute bond for the faithful performance of his duty in this case. Whereupon he,
together with George N. Biggs and S. B. Callen
as his securities who are accepted and approved
by the court, entered into bond, conditioned
according to law, which is ordered to be certified to the Auditor."

33/352 - March 9, 1881 (age 43).
  "We, the jury, impaneled and sworn under
a writ from the Greenup Circuit Court, directing
us to inquire if James and Jacob Steenrod of
Greenup County be of unsound mind, and having
physicians as to their condition that they
could not be brought before the jury, heard
the affidavits of two, and having had evidence
in relation to the condition of their mind
as well as estate, do find that said James
and Jacob Steenrod are idiots, one is about
54 and the other 43 years of age, and that

they have no estate of their own except about
6 1/2 acres, worth $1.50 per acre rent, that
they reside with their married sister, who
have not sufficient estate for one year's maintenance of said idiots; that they were born
in Greenup County, that they are destitute
of mind from their infancy, and that they were
not brought into the state by any person for
the purpose of becoming a charge upon the
Commonwealth, and that they are incapable of
laboring for their own support, and that they
were heretofore found to be idiots by a jury
of Greenup County.
    Given under our hands and seals this 9th
day of March, 1881. (signed) Merdacai Walker."
    NOTE: According to the 1880 Greenup County
Census, the "married sister" is Mary A. Stepter
wife of John Stepter and mother of Isaac
(Isaiah) Stepter.

33/388 - March 17, 1881.
    "It is ordered that John Stepter be appointed
a committee to take charge of said James Steenrod and Jacob Steenrod and provide them with
suitable diet, clothing, etc, and that he be
allowed therefor at the rate of $75.00 per
annum each from the date of the inquest, to
be paid upon the further order of this court.
The said John Stepter, committee as aforesaid,
executed bond to the Commonwealth of Kentucky
as committee aforesaid, conditioned according
to law, which was accepted and approved by
the court, all of which is ordered to be copied
and certified to the Auditor of Public
Accounts."

34/60 - September 1, 1882 (age 49).
    "We, the jury, impaneled and sworn under
a writ from the Greenup Circuit Court directing
us to inquire if Jacob Steenrod of Greenup
County be of unsound mind, and having had a
view of said Jacob Steenrod in open Court,
and having had evidence in relation to the
condition of his mind as well as estate, do
find that said Jacob Steenrod is an idiot;
is about 49 years of age, and that he has no
estate of his own, either in possession,
reversion or remainder; that he resides at

the poorhouse in Greenup County; that he was
born in Greenup County; that he is destitute
of mind from infancy, and that he was not
brought into the state by any person for the
purpose of becoming a charge upon the Commonwealth; and that he is not capable of laboring
in whole or in part for his own support; that
he has heretofore been found an idiot. (signed)
Taylor Warnock.

It is therefore ordered that there be allowed
to clothe and maintain said Jacob Steenrod,
at the rate of $75.00 per annum; and that B.
F. Brown be appointed a committee to clothe
and maintain said Jacob Steenrod. Whereupon
B. F. Brown appeared in court and with D. J.
McCoy as his security, who is accepted and
approved by the court, executed bond as committee aforesaid, conditioned according to
law."

34/117 - March 9, 1883.
"Upon proof of being made to the satisfaction
of the Court that James Steenrod and Jacob
Steenrod heretofore found to be idiots were
alive at the August term 1882 and had not sufficient estate for their support and their parents
were unable to support them, and the committee
for said idiots, John Stepter, having surrendered them to the County Court and no one having
been appointed committee in place of said
Stepter previous to the August term 1882, and
said Greenup County Court having kept, clothed
and maintained said idiots from February term
of the Greenup Circuit Court 1882 until the
August term 1882 thereof, it is ordered by
the Court that Greenup County and the treasurer
thereof be allowed at the rate of $75.00 per
annum each for their support for the time of
the last payment to the former committee, John
Stepter, to the appointment of the present
committee, B. F. Brown, which is ordered to
be certified to the Auditor of Public accounts
for payment."

36/119 - March 1, 1889.
"It appearing to the satisfaction of the
Court that Jacob Steenrod, an idiot, was alive
up to the 12th day of October 1888 in the care

of his committee, and had not sufficient estate
for his support, and that his parents were
unable to support him, it is ordered that the
allowance of $75.00 per annum for his support
be continued from the last payment up to the
12th day of October 1888, and that the same
be certified to the Auditor of Public Accounts,
and it appearing that the committee expended
$10.00 necessary expenses in the burial of
said Jacob Steenrod, it is ordered that he
be allowed $10.00 burial expenses of said idiot,
which is ordered to be certified to the Auditor
for payment."

Steenrod, James: (brother of Jacob Steenrod).
N/441 - April 3, 1844 (age 17).
"On motion of the attorney for the Common-
wealth, it is ordered that the Sheriff of
Greenup County summon twelve housekeepers to
appear here immediately to inquire whether
James Steenrod, who is now in open court, be
or be not of sound mind, and if he be of unsound
mind, whether he was so at the time of his
birth or became so afterwards, and what property
he has and thereupon came a jury, to wit:
Beverly Allen, Stephen Thomas, Joseph Cazell,
Samuel Truitt, John B. Hill, Thomas Lawson,
Jonna D. Glover, William Littlejohn, James
M. Craycraft, Samuel Glover, Noah Anderson,
and Michael Putman, who being elected, tried
and sworn well and truly to inquire into and
ascertain the facts for which they were summoned
to inquire, upon their oaths do say that the
said James Steenrod is an idiot and that he
has been so since his birth; that he is now
about 17 years old and that he has no estate
whatever. That his father is dead and his
mother is alive and hath four small children,
and has not estate to support said idiot.
The said James Steenrod being in open court,
witnesses were examined and counsel appeared.
It is therefore ordered that it be certified
to the Auditor of Public Accounts that Elizabeth
Steenrod, who is appointed to take charge of
the said James Steenrod, is entitled at the
rate of $50.00 per annum from this date for
the use and support of the said James Steenrod."

O/288 - October 27, 1846 (age 18).
  "Upon motion of the attorney for the Commonwealth, it is ordered that a Writ de-idiotio-
inquirendo issue to the case of James Steenrod,
an idiot, returnable immediately to inquire
into the state of mind of said James Steenrod.
And it appearing to the satisfaction of the
Court from the affidavits of Richard W. Morton
and Jeremiah S. Canterbury, two practicing
physicians of this county, that the said James
Steenrod is an idiot, and that it would be
inconvenient to bring him into court, and it
is ordered that L. W. Andrews, Esq., be
appointed counsel for the said James Steenrod.
Whereupon came a jury, to-wit: Cardinal F.
Starke, William Dupuy, Marshall Baker, I. C.
Ferran, Nelson Jones, Charles Craycraft, William
Craycraft, Nelson Pratt, Henry Hardwick, Allen
Myers, Henry Crump, and Nathaniel S. Warner,
who being sworn according to law returned the
following verdict, to-wit: 'We, the jury,
having heard the evidence in relation to the
condition of the mind as well as the estate
and physical ability of said James Steenrod
to perform common labor, do find that said
James Steenrod is about 18 years of age and
has no estate of his own; that he resides with
his parents who have not sufficient estate
for a years maintenance of said James Steenrod;
that he is incapable of preforming common labor,
and that he was not brought into this Commonwealth for the purpose of receiving a support
from the treasury.'
  It is therefore ordered that it be certified
to the Auditor of Public Accounts that Elizabeth
Steenrod, mother of James, the committee of
said James, is entitled at the rate of $50.00
per annum from the 21st day of April 1844 to
this (27 day of October) for the use, support
and maintenance of said James Steenrod."

P/378 - November 1, 1850.
  "In pursuance of an Act of the General
Assembly of Kentucky approved February 21,
1846, requiring inquisitions of idiocy to be
held this year, on Motion of the Attorney for
the Commonwealth it is ordered that a writ
of de idiotia inquirendo issue herein, return-

able immediately, to inquire into the state
of the mind of James Steenrod and whether he
has any estate etc., and L. W. Andrews
volunteered to act as counsel for said James
Steenrod, and the said James Steenrod was
brought into open court, and Jess Poynter,
Reuben Thompson, Carter Allen, Charlten
Shepherd, Geo. W. Darlinton, Silas Greenslate,
Hugh A. Poague, Charles Womack, Mason Greenslate, Thomas Barney, and Henry A. Mead and
Jacob Lawson were empalinelled (sic) sworn
and charged according to law as a jury of
inquest and having heard the evidence returned
the following verdict, towit, 'We, the jury,
find James Steenrod is an idiot, is above twenty
years of age and has no estate; that he resides
with his Mother, his father being dead; that
his Mother has not sufficient estate for a
years maintenance of the said James Steenrod;
that the said James Steenrod has not physical
ability to perform any labor. We further find
that said idiot is a resident of this County
and has not been brought into this state for
the purpose of receiving an allowance from
the Treasury.' It is ordered that the allowance of $50.00 per annum be continued from
the last payment, which is ordered to be certified to the Second Auditor."

R/328 - May 31, 1855 (age 22).
  "We, the jury, find that James Steenrod and
Jacob Steenrod are persons of unsound mind
and idiots; that they were destitute of mind
from infancy; they were born in and reside
in Greenup County and were not brought to this
state for the purpose of becoming a charge
upon the Commonwealth; that their father has
been dead about 10 years and was subject to
fits, and that their mother is still living
in Greenup County, and that she has not sufficient estate to support the said James Steenrod
and Jacob Steenrod; that they are incapable
of laboring in whole or in part for their
support. We further find that James Steenrod
has before been found an idiot, and that no
change has taken place in his mind since the
original inquest, and that Jacob Steenrod has
never been found an idiot. We also find that

said James Steenrod is about 22 years of age
and that said Jacob Steenrod is about 16 years
of age. (signed) Nicholas Savage, Richard Jones,
Jesse Poynter, John C. Burk, Jesse Davidson,
William Craycraft, Carlisle Hunt, Joseph B.
Davidson, George Tanner, Thomas L. Poteet,
Edward Brooks, Alexander Davis.

It is therefore ordered that Elizabeth Steenrod be appointed a committee to take charge
of said James Steenrod and Jacob Steenrod and
provide for them suitable diet, clothing, etc.,
and that she be allowed at the rate of $50.00
per annum from the last allowance for the support of James Steenrod, which is ordered to
be certified to the Auditor for payment and
she is allowed at the rate of $50.00 per annum
from this date to be paid out of the treasury
of this state upon further order of this court."

S/216 - November 15, 1856.
"Elizabeth Steenrod, committee for James
Steenrod and Jacob Steenrod, idiots of this
County, having departed this life since the
last term of this court, it is ordered that
Benj. F. King be appointed a committee for
said idiots, and proof being adduced that said
idiots are in all respects in the same condition in which they were at the last allowance
made to them by this court, it is ordered the
allowance be continued to each of said idiots
and paid to Benj. F. King, their committee,
which is ordered to be certified to the Auditor
of Public Accounts for payment."

U/569 - May 23, 1860 (age 33).
"We, the jury, say that James Steenrod and
Jacob Steenrod, whom we have in charge, are
of unsound mind; that they are idiots. That
they have been destitute of mind from their
birth. Jacob was born in Greenup County,
Kentucky, and is about 21 years old; James
was born in Mason County, Kentucky, and is
about 33 years old or near that, and they have
not been brought into this state for the purpose of becoming a charge upon it; they have
each an undivided interest of 1/6th in about
24 or 25 acres of 2nd or 3rd rate land in this
county worth about a dollar a year rent per

acre, and they have no other estate in possession, reversion or remainder. Their parents
are dead, and the said James and Jacob are
incapable of laboring in whole or in part for
their support. They have before been found,
by the verdict of a jury and Judgment in this
court, idiots, and no change has since taken
place in their minds, physical condition or
estate since the former inquest. (signed) John
T. Lawson.

It is therefore adjuged by the Court that
James and Jacob Steenrod are idiots and Benjamin
F. King, their former committee, having tendered
his resignation in writing. It is ordered
that Moses F. Dupuy be appointed to take charge
of said James and Jacob Steenrod, and provide
for them suitable diet, clothing, etc., and
that the allowance of $50.00 per annum each
be continued from the last payment, which is
ordered to be certified to the Auditor.

It is further ordered that said Moses F.
Dupuy gave bond and security, for the faithful
performance of his duties in the penalty of
$200.00. Whereupon he, together with George
E. Roe as his security, executed bond according-
ly, which is approved by the court."

X/458 - September 5, 1865 (age 33).
"We, the jury, find that James Steenrod,
the person under charge, is an idiot, and that
he has been destitute of mind from infancy.
He was born in this state and has always lived
in this state, and is 33 years of age. He
is the owner of 1/6th of 24 acres of land,
which 24 acres of land is worth $60.00 per
year rent. His parents are dead. He is not
capable of laboring in whole or in part for
his support. He was found to be an idiot by
a former inquest in this court. (Signed) Lewis
Nicholls.

And the court being satisfied with the
inquest adjudges that the said James Steenrod
is an idiot and has not sufficient estate for
his support, and his parents are unable to
support him. It is therefore ordered that
the sum of $50.00 per annum be allowed for
his support and maintenance from the last allowance, payable to James Bryan, his committee."

<u>NOTE</u>: James is referred to as 33 years
of age at both U/569 and X/458.

26/144 - September 7, 1870 (age 43).
   "We, the jury, find that James Steenrod,
whom we have in charge, is an idiot and has
been destitute of mind from infancy; that his
father and mother are both dead; that he was
born in Kentucky and has lived here ever since;
that he is in his 43 year; that he has no estate
in possession, reversion or remainder, except
3 acres of 3rd rate land on Tygarts Creek in
Greenup County, which is not sufficient for
his support, and he is incapable of laboring
for his support, either in part or in whole,
and that he has heretofore been found an idiot
by a verdict of a jury, and a Judgment of this
court. (signed) Lewis Nicholls, foreman.
   And it is, therefore, ordered that John
Stepter be continued as committee to take charge
of said James Steenrod and provide him with
suitable diet, clothing, etc. and that he be
allowed therefor at the rate of $50.00 per
annum from the last payment, to be paid upon
the further order of this court, which is
ordered to be certified to the Auditor."

31/22 - September 6, 1875.
   "We, the jury, find from the evidence that
the defendant, James Steenrod, is an idiot;
that he was born in Greenup County, Kentucky
about 1827 and has always lived in said County;
that he has no estate to support him except
4 1/4 acres of land in said County worth about
$12.00 per acre, in possession, reversion or
remainder; that his parents are dead and left
no estate except the above named and that he
is not capable of laboring to any extent for
his support; that he has heretofore been found
an idiot; that said land is of no value to
him after paying for keeping up the repairs.
(signed) Geo. W. Callihan.
   And it is therefore ordered that John Stepter
be appointed a committee to take charge of
said James Steenrod and provide him with suitable diet, clothing, etc., and that he be
allowed therefor at the rate of $75.00 per
annum from this date. It is further ordered

that John Stepter give bond and security, conditioned according to law, for the faithful
performance of his duty in this case, and thereupon he appeared in court with George N. Biggs
and S. B. Callen as his securities and executed
bond according to this order, and the same
was accepted and ordered to be certified to
the Auditor."

33/352- March 9, 1881 (age 54).
"We, the jury, impaneled and sworn under
a writ from the Greenup Circuit Court, directing
us to inquire if James and Jacob Steenrod of
Greenup County be of unsound mind, and having
physicians as to their condition that they
could not be brought before the jury, heard
the affidavits of two and having had evidence
in relation to the condition of their mind
as well as estate, do find that said James
and Jacob Steenrod are idiots, one is about
54 and the other 43 years of age, and that
they have no estate of their own except about
6 1/2 acres, worth $1.50 per acre rent, that
they reside with their married sister, who
have not sufficient estate for one year's maintenance of said idiots; that they were born
in Greenup County; that they are destitute
of mind from their infancy, and that they were
not brought into the state by any person for
the purpose of becoming a charge upon the
Commonwealth, and that they are incapable of
laboring for their own support, and that they
were heretofore found to be idiots by a jury
of Greenup County.
    Given under our hands and seals this 9th
day of March, 1881. (signed) Merdacai Walker."
    NOTE: According to the 1880 Greenup County
Census, the "married sister" is Mary A. Stepter,
wife of John Stepter and mother of Isaac
(Isaiah) Stepter.

33/388 - March 17, 1881.
    "It is ordered that John Stepter be appointed
a committee to take charge of said James Steenrod and Jacob Steenrod and provide them with
suitable diet, clothing, etc, and that he be
allowed therefor at the rate of $75.00 per
annum each from the date of the inquest, to

be paid upon the further order of this court.
The said John Stepter, committee as aforesaid,
executed bond to the Commonwealth of Kentucky
as committee aforesaid, conditioned according
to law, which was accepted and approved by
the court, all of which is ordered to be copied
and certified to the Auditor of Public
Accounts."

34/60 - September 1, 1882 (age 53).
  "We, the jury, empaneled (sic) and sworn
under a writ from the Greenup Circuit Court
directing us to inquire if James Steenrod of
Greenup County, Kentucky, be of unsound mind,
and having had a view of said James Steenrod
in open court, and having had evidence in
relation to his mind and estate, do find that
said James Steenrod is an idiot; is about 53
years of age, and that he has no estate in
possession, reversion, or remainder; that he
resides in the poorhouse, Greenup County; that
he was born in Greenup County; that he was
destitute of mind from infancy, and that he
was not brought into the state by any person
for the purpose of becoming a charge upon the
Commonwealth, and that he is incapable of laboring in whole or in part for his support; that
he has heretofore been found an idiot. (signed)
Taylor Warnock.
  It is therefore ordered that said James
Steenrod be allowed at the rate of $75.00 per
year for his maintenance, and that B. F. Brown
be appointed a committee to take charge of
said James Steenrod and clothe and maintain
him. Whereupon said Brown appeared in court
and with D. J. McCoy as his surety, who is
accepted and approved, executed bond according
to law."

34/87 - March 1, 1883.
  "It appearing to the satisfaction of the
Court that James Steenrod, an idiot, was up
to the 18th day of February 1883 alive in the
care of his committee, and that he was unable
to labor in whole or in part for his support,
and that his parents were still unable to support him, it is ordered that the allowance
of $75.00 per annum be continued from the

inquest of the jury herein up to the 18th day
of February 1883, which is ordered to be copied
and certified to the auditor for payment."

"It appearing to the satisfaction of the
Court that James Steenrod, an idiot, died on
the 18th day of February 1883, departed this
life and was buried by B. F. Brown, his committee, it is ordered that said committee be
allowed $10.00 for burial expenses, which is
ordered to be copied and certified to the
auditor for payment."

34/117 - March 9, 1883.
"Upon proof of being made to the satisfaction
of the Court that James Steenrod and Jacob
Steenrod heretofore found to be idiots were
alive at the August term 1882, and had not
sufficient estate for their support, and their
parents were unable to support them, and the
committee for said idiots, John Stepter, having
surrendered them to the County Court and no
one having been appointed committee in place
of said Stepter previous to the August term
1882, and said Greenup County Court having
kept, clothed and maintained said idiots from
February term of the Greenup Circuit Court
1882 until the August term 1882 thereof, it
is ordered by the Court that Greenup County
and the treasurer thereof be allowed at the
rate of $75.00 per annum each for their support
for the time of the last payment to the former
committee, John Stepter, to the appointment
of the present committee, B. F. Brown, which
is ordered to be certified to the Auditor of
Public Accounts for payment."

34/171 - August 25, 1884.
"It appearing to the satisfaction of the court
that James Steenrod, an idiot, is still alive,
in the care of his committee, and has not sufficient estate for his support, and that his
parents are unable to support him, it is ordered
that the allowance of $75.00 per annum be con-
tinued from the last payment, which is ordered
to be certified to the Auditor for payment."
    NOTE: I believe this entry should read
Jacob instead of James, as Jacob died October
12, 1888 and James died February 18, 1883.

Stepter, Isaiah (Isaah):
(nephew of Jacob and James Steenrod)
37/74 - April 4, 1893.
    "It appearing to the satisfaction of the
court that Amos Carr and Isaiah Stepter, idiots,
are still alive, and in the care of their committees, and have not sufficient estate for
their support, and that their parents are still
unable to support them, it is ordered that
the allowance of $75.00 per annum be continued
from the finding of the jury and that the same
be certified to the Auditor of Public Accounts."

37/139 - July 19, 1893.
    "It appearing to the satisfaction of the
Court that Isaah Stepter, an idiot, is alive
and has not sufficient estate for his support,
and that his parents are still unable to support
him, it is ordered that the allowance of $75.00
per annum be continued from the last payment
and the same be certified to the Auditor. J.
Watt Womack, committee for said Isaah Stepter,
tendered his resignation which was accepted.
Ordered that said J. Watt Womack be paid the
amount due said idiot up to the present term
of Court. Ordered that Lavenia R. Wade be
appointed committee for said Isaiah Stepter."

39/500 - July 24, 1902.
    "Inquests were this day held upon Amos Carr,
Lavinia Flannigan and Isaiah Stepter and
recorded."

Stump, Nancy:
N/291 - April 4, 1843.
    "On motion of the attorney for the Common-
wealth, it is ordered that a Writ of De idiota
inquirendo issue, returnable immediately, to
inquire into the state of the mind of Nancy
Stump, who was found to be an idiot at a former
term of this court, and whether she has any
estate etc., and it is ordered that L. W.
Andrews, Esq., be appointed counsel for the
said Nancy Stump. Whereupon the said Nancy
Stump was brought into court and Charles Craycraft, Johnson G. Glover, Job Davis, John E.
Winn, Henry Harding, Abraham Brooks, James
Bryan, Nathaniel S. Warner, George W. Darlinton,

Walter Smiley, Allen Myers, and William Bussell
were empannelled (sic), sworn and charged
according to law, returned the following
verdict, viz: 'On motion of the Attorney for
the Commonwealth, it is ordered that the Sheriff
of Greenup County summon twelve housekeepers
of this County to appear here immediately to
inquire whether Nancy Stump, who is now in
open court, be or not of sound mind, and if
she be of unsound mind, whether she was so
from the time of her birth or become so afterwards, and what property she has, and thereupon
came a jury towit, Levi I. Hampton, Silas
Woodard, John Kizer, Clem Swearingin, Nathaniel
Davis, Horatio Catlett, William Hampton, Griffin
T. Roach, A. A. Clutz, Ralph St. John, Cornelius
Anderson and Joseph Ewing, who being elected,
tried and sworn well and truly to inquire into
and ascertain the facts of which they were
summoned to enquire (sic), upon their oaths
do say that the said Nancy Stump is an idiot,
and that she has been so since her birth, and
that she hath no estate whatever.' The said
Nancy was in open court, witnesses were examined
and counsel appeared.
   It is therefore ordered that it be
certified to the Auditor of Public Accounts
that Nancy Smith, who is appointed a committee
to take care of the said Nancy Stump, is
entitled at the rate of $50.00 per annum from
this date for the use and support of said Nancy
Stump."

N/350 - October 3, 1843.
   "It appearing to the Court from the evidence
of George W. Smith, that Nancy Stump, who was
found to be an idiot at the last term of this
Court, still lives and continues in the same
situation.
   It is therefore ordered that it be
certified to the Auditor of Public Accounts
that Nancy Smith, the committee of said Nancy
Stump, is entitled to receive at the rate of
$50.00 per annum from the 4th day of April
1843 to the present time (October 3, 1843)
for the use and support of said Nancy Stump."

O/384 - May 1, 1847 (age 18).

"We, the jury, find that said Nancy Stump
is an idiot, is about 18 years of age and has
no estate; that she resides with Nancy Smith,
her parents being dead, leaving no estate whatsoever; that said Nancy Stump has not the
physical ability to perform any labor. We
further find that said idiot is a resident
and was born in the County.

It is therefore ordered that Nancy Smith,
the committee of said Nancy Stump, and who
is continued as such, be allowed at the rate
of $50.00 per annum from the 8th day of October
1845 to this date (May 1, 1847) to be paid
out of the treasury of this state for the use,
support and maintenance of said Nancy Stump,
which is ordered to be certified to the Second
Auditor."

P/474 - May 1, 1851 (age 22).
"In pursuance of an Act of the General Assembly
of the Commonwealth of Kentucky approved
February 21, 1856, requiring inquisitions of
idiotcy to be held in the present year.

It is on Motion of the Attorney for the
Commonwealth ordered that a writ of de idiota
inquirendo issue, returnable immediately, to
inquire into the state of mind of Nancy Stump
and whether she has any estate etc, and it
is ordered that L. W. Andrews, Esq., be
appointed counsel for the said Nancy Stump.
Whereupon the said Nancy Stump personally
appeared in court. And William Dupuy, Reuben
Thompson, Jesse L. Dupuy, William Bryson,
Richard Jones, Silas Greenslate, Lucus M. Higby,
A. L. Reid, James Morton, Rival D. Jones, James
Meek, Benjamin F. Lawson were empannelled (sic),
sworn and charged according to law, as a jury
of inquest under said writ and having heard
the evidence returned the following verdict
towit, 'We, the jury, find the said Nancy Stump
is an idiot; is about twenty two years of age;
that she has no parents living, that she has
not the physical ability to perform any labor;
that she was born in and still continues a
resident of this county.'

It is therefore ordered that John W. Smith
administrator of Nancy Smith, deceased, the
former committee of said Nancy Stump, be allowed

at the rate of $50.00 per annum from the last
allowance up to the 25th day of November last.
It is further ordered that William B. Smith
be appointed a committee to take charge of
the said Nancy Stump and that the allowance
of $50.00 per annum for her support be paid
him from the 25th day of November last, which
is ordered to be certified to the Second
Auditor."

R/285 - May 29, 1855 (age 30)
    "We, the jury, find that said Nancy Stump
is an idiot; about 30 years of age and has
no estate; that her parents are dead and have
left no estate whatever. That the said Nancy
Stump was born in and is a citizen of Greenup
County and has not been brought into this state
for the purpose of receiving a support out
of the treasury. We further find that the
said Nancy Stump has not the physical ability
to perform any labor for her support; that
she has before been found by verdict of a jury
an idiot; that no change has taken place in
her mind, physical condition or estate since
the original inquest.
    It is therefore ordered that William R.
Smith be appointed a committee to take charge
of said Nancy Stump and to provide for her
suitable diet, clothing, etc., and that he
be allowed therefor at the rate of $50.00 per
annum from the last allowance, which is ordered
to be certified to the Auditor of Public
Accounts for payment."

V/192 - November 19, 1860 (age 30).
    "We, the jury, find that Nancy Stump is an
idiot; that she was born in Greenup County
and has always resided in said county. That
she is about 30 years of age, that her parents
are both dead; that she has no property in
possession, remainder, or revision sufficient
for her support and that she is not capable
of laboring in whole or in part for her maintenance, that she has heretofore by the verdict
of a jury and a judgment of this court been
found an idiot, and that no change in her mind,
physical condition or estate has taken place
since the original inquest. (signed) B. F.
Bennett, foreman.

It is therefore adjudged by the court that
the said Nancy Stump is an idiot, and it is
ordered that the allowance of $50.00 per annum
be continued to her from the last payment."

X/497- September 9, 1865.
"We, the jury, find that Nancy Stump, the
person under charge, is of unsound mind and
is not an idiot; that she was born in Greenup
County, Kentucky and has always lived in the
state. That she has no estate of any kind.
Her parents are dead. She is not capable of
laboring in whole or in part for her support.
(signed) James Sutherland.
And the court being satisfied with the
inquest of the jury adjudges that the said
Nancy Stump is of unsound mind and not an
idiot."

Tisdale, Sytha:
38/266 - April 8, 1898.
"An inquest was this day held upon Sytha
Tisdale, a lunatic, and recorded."

Traylor, Bertha (Birdie):
37/444 - November 7, 1895.
"It appearing to the satisfaction of the
court that Mary Wheeler, John Wood and Jennie
Belle Smith, lunatics, and Gracie Guilkey,
Bertha Traylor, Minnie McGinnis, Celia Leathers,
Did Nicholls, Grant Damarin, Amos Carr, Isaiah
Stepter, Lucy Middaugh, John Smith, John
Traylor, Minta Traylor and Cordelia Caywood,
idiots, are still alive in the care of their
committees, and have not sufficient estate
for their support and that their parents are
still unable to support them, it is ordered
that the allowance of $75.00 per annum each
for their support be continued from the last
payment, and that the same be certified to
the Auditor for payment."

39/368 - November 7, 1901.
"It appearing to the satisfaction of the
Court that Gracie Guilkey, Hannah Davis, Ella
Jennings, Birdie Traylor, William C. Kitts,
James A. Kitts, Bennie Adkins, John Murphy,
and Martha Wadkins, idiots, are still alive,

in the care of their committees and have not
sufficient estate for their support, and that
their parents are still unable to support them,
it is ordered that the allowance of $75.00
per annum each for their support be continued
from the last payment, and that the same be
copied and certified to the Auditor of Public
Accounts for payment."

Traylor, John:
37/365 - April 5, 1895.
"Inquests were this day held upon Minnie
McGinnis, Rebecca Traylor and John Traylor,
idiots, and recorded."

39/383 - November 11, 1901.
"It appearing to the satisfaction of the
court that Mary Wheeler and John Wood, lunatics,
and Amos Carr, Cynthia Ann Burton, Minta
Traylor, John Traylor, Lucy Middaugh, Did
Nicholls, Isaiah Stepter, Minnie McGinnis,
and Mary Griffith, idiots, are still alive,
in the care of their committees, and have not
estate sufficient for their support, and that
their parents are still unable to support them."

Traylor, Minta (Mintie):
37/418 - July 20, 1895.
"An inquest was this day held upon Minta
Traylor, an idiot, and recorded."

39/383 - November 11, 1901.
"It appearing to the satisfaction of the
court that Mary Wheeler and John Wood, lunatics,
and Amos Carr, Cynthia Ann Burton, Minta
Traylor, John Traylor, Lucy Middaugh, Did
Nicholls, Isaiah Stepter, Minnie McGinnis,
and Mary Griffith, idiots, are still alive,
in the care of their committees, and have not
estate sufficient for their support, and that
their parents are still unable to support them."

Traylor, Rebecca:
37/365 - April 5, 1895.
"Inquests were this day held upon Minnie
McGinnis, Rebecca Traylor and John Traylor
and recorded."

Tufts (Tuffs, Tuffts), Aaron:
(brother of Margaret Lacey)
I/73 - October 5, 1832.
   "On motion of the attorney for the Commonwealth, the Clerk is directed to issue a Writ
of Deidiota Inquirendo, returnable immediately,
to inquire into the state of mind and estate
of Aaron Tuffs, who is now in court, and the
Court waiving the necessity of a writ, it is
ordered that Willam Conner be appointed to
attend the trial for lunacy and see that said
Tuffs be not improperly condemned, and thereupon
a jury was impannelled (sic) as follows, towit:
Bazil Waring, John F_____, Squire Barney,
John Baligee, Andrew Hood, Jr., Philip B. Hord,
John N. Ward, John W. Shropshire, Allen
Campbell, John Dorch, and Andrew Locker, and
John D. Williams, who being sworn as the law
directs, well and truly to inquire into the
state of mind and precuniary circumstances
of said Aaron Tuffs, after hearing the evidence
adduced, signed the following verdict, towit:
'We, the Jury, find that Aaron Tuff is a lunatic
and that he has become so since his birth;
that said Tuff is possessed of some estate
real and personal the value of which is not
ascertained.' And therefore it is ordered
that James Stewart and John Culvursan be
appointed a committee for said Tuff to do with
him and his estate as the law directs."

I/106 - April 4, 1833.
   "It appearing to the satisfaction of the
court that Aaron Tuffs who was at a former
term of this court found to be a lunatick (sic)
is restored and is now of sound mind. It is
ordered that the order appointing James Stewart
and John Culbertson a committee for said Tuffs
at the last October term be and the same is
hereby set aside."

R/186 - December 1, 1854 (age 36).
   "We, the jury, impaneled and sworn under
a writ from the Greenup Circuit Court directing
us to inquire if Aaron Tufts of Greenup County
be of unsound mind, and having had a view of
said Aaron Tufts in open court and having heard
evidence in relation to the condition of his

mind as well as estate do find that said Aaron
Tufts is a lunatic, is about 36 years of age,
was born in the State of Ohio, has lived in
what is now Greenup County, Kentucky, for some
32 years. That his father is now deceased,
was a lunatic, that one of his sisters, Mrs.
Lacee, is now in the Lunatic Asylum at
Lexington, Kentucky. That one other of his
sisters is insane, that said Aaron is insane
upon the subject of religion. That his insanity
commenced in the Fall of 1848. We also find
that said Aaron Tufts resides with his Mother
in Greenup County; never was married; that
his only estate consists of a reversionary
interest of one undivided eighth of one 130
acres of land lying in Greenup County valued
at $6.00 per acre. That interest depending
upon the death of Aaron's mother. Given under
our hands and seals this 1st day of December
1854.
     The first evident insanity which was dis-
covered in Mr. Tufts was in the year 1848.
All the evidence introduced relative to the
cause of his lunacy tended to prove that it
was hereditary. His father was deranged in
advanced life and he has a sister now in the
asylum at Lexington. There is no evidence
of any disease by and some degree of physical
depreciation necessarily resulting from the
mental derangement. I cannot therefore state
that there existed any other cause for his
insanity than that mysterious and bitter inheri-
tance which seems to have been transmitted
to him from his paternal ancestry; that the
Superintendent of the asylum will learn from
the verdict that his insanity has uniformly
been in reference to religion. Given under
my hand as presiding Judge of the Greenup
Circuit Court this 1st day of December 1854.
(signed) J. Moore"
     NOTE: If the above paragraph is correct
in that Aaron Tufts first showed signs of lunacy
in 1848, then is it possible that entries I/73
and I/106 are for his father? If so, then
the entry of 7/100 would make sense.
     7/100 - March 1, 1841 - Wealthy Ann Tuffts
obtained letters for administration of the
estate of her deceased husband, Aaron Tuffts.

7/223 - January 1, 1844 - Wealthy Ann Tuffts
is now Wealthy Ann Norman.

Vandergriff, William:
39/372 - November 8, 1901.
"It appearing to the satisfaction of the
court that Martha Jasper and Mary Clutts,
lunatics, and John Lawson, Christina McFarland,
William Vandergriff, Caroline Ham, Cora Horner,
Lavinia Flannigan, idiots, are still alive,
in the care of their committees and have not
estate sufficient for their support, and that
their parents are still unable to support them,
it is ordered that the allowance of $75.00
per annum each for their support be continued
from the last payment, and that the same be
copied and certified to the Auditor of Public
Accounts for payment."

Walker, George P.:
17/213 - May 26, 1886.
"It appearing to the satisfaction of the
court from the record of the inquest in the
case of George P. Walker, a lunatic, and proof
heard that the said George P. Walker is a
lunatic and now confined in the asylum and
incompetent to manage his estate, it is ordered
that Helen M. Walker be and she is hereby
appointed a committee to take charge of the
estate of said George P. Walker, a lunatic,
and have the care and custody of same; and
it further appearing to the satisfaction of
the court that the sale of certain lands or
minerals underlying the same to the Cambria
Iron Company in the County of Fayette and State
of Pennsylavania in which said George P. Walker
has an interest would _____ to the advantage
of the estate of said lunatic, it is therefore
considered that said Helen M. Walker, committee
of said George P. Walker, a lunatic, be and
she is hereby authorized and empowered to
execute and deliver to the said Cambria Iron
Company for and on behalf of said George P.
Walker, a lunatic, such deed or deeds as shall
be necessary to convey to the said company
any or all the interest of said George P. Walker
in and to said lands and minerals underlying
the same or either, and to give such receipts

and acquittances as shall be necessary in the
execution of said deeds and remove and hold
the funds arising from such sales and transfers
as committee aforesaid subject to the orders
of the court.

Whereupon the said Helen M. Walker, committee
for said lunatic, appeared in court and together
with William Walker and Joseph Savage as her
sureties, who are accepted and approved by
the court, executed bond to the Commonwealth
of Kentucky as committee aforesaid, conditioned
according to law. (signed) Lewis Nicholls,
Presiding Judge"

18/129 - May 18, 1888.
"Ordered that James D. Biggs be and he is
hereby appointed committee of the estate of
George P. Walker, a lunatic. Whereupon he
appeared in Court and took the oath required
by law, and together with Joseph Savage and
J. B. Hockaday as his sureties, who are accepted
and approved by the Court, executed bond to
the Commonwealth of Kentucky, as committee
aforesaid conditioned according to law."

26/140 - March 5, 1889.
"Ordered that James D. Biggs be appointed
committee for George P. Walker, a lunatic.
Whereupon he appeared in court and took the
oath required by law, and with Lewis Nicholls
as his surety, who is accepted and approved
by the court executed bond as committee aforesaid, conditioned according to law."

37/59 - September 9, 1892.
"Upon proof heard in open court, it is ordered
that said J. D. Biggs, Committee of G. P.
Walker, expend $200.00 of the principal of
the trust funds in his hands for the board
and tuition of the minor children of said
Walker.

Before this time, upon proof in open court,
the court ordered said committee to expend
$100.00 for the same purpose for which this
$200.00 is ordered expended, but no order was
entered, but it is now done for then."

Walker, James B.:

31/196 - March 6, 1876 (age 20).
"Upon motion of the attorney for the Commonwealth, it is ordered that a writ of de idota
inquirendo issue in the case of James B. Walker,
an idiot, returnable immediately, to inquire
into the state of mind of said Walker, and
it is ordered that Edward F. Dulin, Esq., be
appointed counsel for said Walker. Whereupon
came a jury, towit: Robert Johnson, Jacob
Anderson, Frank Waring, T. J. Thompson, Lewis
Nicholls, Harvey Hodge, H. J. McAllister, John
A. Smith, Moses Pickens, George Gammon, T.
J. Loper, Seymour Harding, who were duly sworn,
and having heard the evidence returned the
following verdict: 'We the jury impanelled
and sworn to inquire to the state of mind of
James B. Walker do find as follows:
    His name is James B. Walker. He was 20
years old last December, was born in Greenup
County, Kentucky, resides in Greenup County,
Kentucky. He is single, never married, has
no children. His occupation is farming. He
did never use ardent spirits, opium or tobacco
in excess. He has been in the condition and
state of mind since 1st January 1876. It came
on gradually like. His general health has
been very good until last fall; he had a severe
attack of sickness, a kind of congestive chill
with severe fever, since then his health has
been delicate. He never was insane before
and never showed any symptoms of a diseased
mind. There has been no change, the disease
seems to be stationary. There are no leud
intervals, at times a little better, at other
times not so well. Never attempted any self
injury. Not inclined to tear clothes or break
furniture, no disposition to injure others.
He is attentive to the calls of nature. The
spell of sickness spoken of is supposed to
be the exciting cause of his malady. No knowledge that any relative of said Walker, on
the father's or mother's side was insane. Not
subject to anything like epelepsey (sic) or
palsey. He has not been subject to any mechan-
ical restraint, he has not estate in property
of any kind except a horse worth $100.00. He
is not in condition to labor in whole or in
part for his support. His parents are alive

and reside in Greenup County, Kentucky, and
have estate enough to take care and provide
for him. He is insane, this is shown from
his unusual and incoherent talk and conduct.'
(signed) Robt. Johnson.

It is therefore considered by the Court
that the said James B. Walker is insane and
that James Walker, Sr. be appointed a committee
to convey him to the asylum."

Waring, James W.:
I/176 - April 7, 1834 (age 33).

"On motion of the attorney for the Commonwealth, the Clerk is directed to issue a Writ
de idiota inquirendo, returnable immediately,
to inquire into the state of mind and estate
of James W. Waring, who is now in court, and
the court waving the necessity of a Writ,
assigned Francis L. Hord as counsel to attend
to the trial for lunacy and see that said James
W. Waring be not improperly condemned, and
thereupon a jury was impanelled, who being
sworn well and truly to inquire into the state
of mind and estate of said Waring, after considering the evidence returned the following
verdict: 'We the jury find that James W. Waring
is a lunatic; that he was 33 years old last
October and became a lunatic about 7 years
since, shortly after a spell of fever and has
no estate out of which to support'"

Waring, Tabitha:
17/119 - December 19, 1881.

"It appearing to the satisfaction of the
court from proof introduced that Tabitha Waring
is incompetent to manage her estate on account
of imbecility and unsoundness of mind, it is
ordered that S. H. Carnegy be appointed a committee to take care and custody of the person
and estate of said Tabitha Waring.

Whereupon he appeared in court and took
the oath required by law, and with James Cliften
as his surety, who is accepted and approved,
executed bond to the Commonwealth of Kentucky
as committee aforesaid, conditioned according
to law."

Watkins, Martha:

39/71 - November 9, 1899.
"It appearing to the satisfaction of the
court that Mary Clutts, Mary Wheeler, Jennie
Belle Smith, and John Wood, lunatics, and Ella
Jennings, Bennie Adkins, John Murphy, Martha
Wadkins, William C. Kitts, James A. Kitts,
Bertha Traylor, George Wurts, Cynthia Ann
Burton, Amos Carr, William Friley, Mary
Griffith, Celia Leathers, Minnie McGinnis,
Lucy Middaugh, Did Nicholls, John Traylor,
Mintie Traylor, Isaiah Stepter, and Hannah
Davis, idiots, are still alive, in the care
of their committees, and have not estate sufficient for their support, and that their parents
are still unable to support them, it is ordered
that the allowance of $75.00 per annum each
for their support be continued from the last
payment and that the same be copied and certified to the Auditor of Public Accounts for
payment."

39/368 - November 7, 1901.
"It appearing to the satisfaction of the
Court that Gracie Guilkey, Hannah Davis, Ella
Jennings, Birdie Traylor, William C. Kitts,
James A. Kitts, Bennie Adkins, John Murphy,
and Martha Wadkins, idiots, are still alive,
in the care of their committees and have not
sufficient estate for their support, and that
their parents are still unable to support them,
it is ordered that the allowance of $75.00
per annum each for their support be continued
from the last payment, and that the same be
copied and certified to the Auditor of Public
Accounts for payment."

Wheeler, Mary:
36/93 - February 26, 1889 (age 35).
"To Hon. A. E. Cole, Judge of the Greenup
Circuit Court: I am reliably informed that
Mary Wheeler is a person of unsound mind and
therefore ask that a jury be impaneled to pass
upon the subject. (signed) James H. Sallee,
Commonwealth Attorney, 14th Judicial Dist.
Ordered by the court that Thomas H. Paynter,
Esq., an attorney of this court, be and he
is hereby appointed to defend for and on behalf
of the person under trial to inquire, comes

a jury, to-wit: J. F. Taylor, T. O. Thompson,
Charles Stewart, James Logan, Gale Messer,
James H. Savage, William Gordon, G. G. Nicholls,
C. J. Forts, W. W. Warnock, C. W. Callihan,
John S. Morgan, who being duly elected and
sworn according to law, after hearing the
evidence and having a view of said Mary Wheeler
in open court, returned the following verdict,
viz: 'We, the jury, find from the evidence
that Mary Wheeler is a person of unsound mind
and a lunatic and that the cause of the unsoundness of mind is not known; that she was born
in Greenup County, Kentucky, and resides in
Greenup County, Kentucky, and is about 35 years
old, and that she was not brought into this
State for the purpose of becoming a charge
upon the Commonwealth; that she owns no estate
of any kind, in possession, reversion or
remainder; that her father is dead and mother
dead, and resided in, and left no estate sufficient to support the person under trial and
said Mary Wheeler is not capable of laboring
in whole or in part for her support; that she
has not heretofore been adjudged a lunatic.'
(signed) C. J. Forts, foreman.
     And it is therefore ordered that J. Watt
Womack be appointed a committee to take charge
of said Mary Wheeler and provide her with suitable diet, clothing, etc., and that he be
allowed therefor at the rate of $75.00 per
annum from this date to be paid upon the further
order of this court."

36/175 - August 27, 1889.
     "J. Watt Womack, committee for Mary Wheeler,
appeared in Court and with W. B. Taylor as
his security, who is accepted and approved
by the court, executed bond to the Commonwealth of Kentucky as committee aforesaid,
conditioned according to law.
     Upon proof of being made to the satisfaction
of the court that Mary Wheeler, heretofore
found to be an idiot, is still alive in the
care of her committee, and has not sufficient
estate for her support, and that her parents
are still unable to support her, it is ordered
that J. Watt Womack, her committee be allowed
at the rate of $75.00 per annum for her support

from the finding of the jury at a former term
of this Court to this date, which is ordered
to be certified to the Auditor of Public
Accounts."

39/383 - November 11, 1901.
"It appearing to the satisfaction of the
court that Mary Wheeler and John Wood, lunatics,
and Amos Carr, Cynthia Ann Burton, Minta
Traylor, John Traylor, Lucy Middaugh, Did
Nicholls, Isaiah Stepter, Minnie McGinnis,
and Mary Griffith, idiots, are still alive,
in the care of their committees, and have not
estate sufficient for their support, and that
their parents are still unable to support them."

Williams, Harrison (Harrisen):
33/315 - March 3, 1881 (age 38).
"Upon the motion of the attorney for the
Commonwealth is ordered that a writ de idiota
inquiredo issue in the case of Harrisen
Williams, an idiot, returnable immediately,
to inquire into the state of mind of the said
Harrisen Williams, and it is ordered that B.
F. Bennett, Esq., be appointed counsel for
said Harrisen Williams, whereupon came a jury,
towit: George Brown, William Gilley, Andy
Verbiek, Robert Stevensen, N. C. MacKoy,
Johathan Callihan, W. B. Smith, Jesse Campbell,
William Walker, George W. Davissin, George
Wills, and H. C. Morton, who being sworn according to law, returned the following verdict,
towit: We, the jury, impannelled (sic) and
sworn under a writ from the Greenup Circuit
Court, directing us to inquire if Harrisen
Williams of Greenup County, be of unsound mind,
and having had a view of said Harrisen Williams
in open court, and having had evidence in relation to the condition of his mind as well
as his estate, do find that said Harrisen
Williams is an idiot; is about 38 years of
age; and that he has no estate of his own;
that he resides with his sister; and that his
father is dead and his mother is living, who
has not sufficient estate for one years maintenance of said Williams; that he was born in
Carter County, Kentucky; that he was destitute
of mind from his infancy, and that he was not

brought into the state by any person for the
purpose of becoming a charge upon the Commonwealth, and that he is incapable of laboring
for his own support in whole or in part.

Given under our hands and seals, this 3rd
day of March, 1881. (signed) H. C. Morton,
seal"

33/398 - August 22, 1881.
"Ordered that Merdacai Walker be appointed
committee for Harrison Willams, an idiot. He
thereupon appeared in court and with W. F.
McD___vell, as his security, who is accepted
and approved by the court, executed bond as
committee aforesaid, conditioned according
to law.

Upon proof being made to the satisfaction
of the court that Harrison Williams, herefore
found to be an idiot, is still alive in the
care of Merdacai Walker, his committee, and
has not sufficient estate for his support,
and his parents are unable to support him,
it is ordered by the court that Merdacai Walker,
his committee, be allowed at the rate of $75.00
per annum for his support from the finding
of the jury at a former term of this court
to this date, which is ordered to be certified
to the Auditor of Public Accounts for payment."

34/48 - August 30, 1882 (age 40).
"Upon proof being made to the satisfaction
of the court, that Harrison Williams heretofore found to be an idiot, is about 40 years
of age and that he has no estate of his own;
that he resides with his mother, who has not
sufficient estate for one years maintenance
of said Harrison Williams; that he was born
in Carter County. We of the jury impaneled
and sworn under a writ from the Greenup Circuit
Court directing us to inquire if Harrisen
Williams of Greenup County be of unsound mind,
and having had a view of said Harrisen Williams
in open court, and having had evidence in
relation to the condition of his mind as well
as estate, do find that the said Harrison
Williams is an idiot. It is therefore ordered
that an allowance of $75.00 per year for the
support and maintenance of said Harrison

Williams be made; that Merdacai Walker be
appointed a committee to take care of said
idiot and maintain, clothe and support him;
that he was destitute of mind from infancy,
and that he was not brought into the state
by any person for the purpose of becoming a
charge upon the Commonwealth, and that he is
incapable of laboring for his own support and
has heretofore been found to be an idiot.
(signed) Jacob Barney.
    The said M. Walker appeared in court and
with Robert Johnson as his security, who is
accepted and approved by the court, executed
bond to the Commonwealth of Kentucky as required
by law."

34/171 - August 25, 1884.
    "It appearing to the satisfaction of the
court that Harrison Williams is still alive
and was in the care of his committee up to
the 10th day of June, 1884, and had not sufficient estate for his support and his parents
were unable to support him. It is ordered
that the allowance of $75.00 per annum for
his support be continued from the last payment
to the said 10th day of June 1884, which is
ordered to be copied and certified to the
auditor for payment."

Wills, William M.:
38/404 - November 11, 1898.
    "An inquest was this day held upon William
M. Wills, a lunatic and recorded."

Wilson, Elizabeth:
18/202 - October 7, 1889.
    "Elizabeth Wilson appeared in Court and moved
the court to appoint a committee to manage
her estate, and proof being heard, and the
court being sufficiently advised adjudges that
the said Elizabeth Wilson, on account of infirm-
ity and the weight of age, is rendered incompetent to manage her estate.
    It is therefore ordered that Thomas M. Biggs
be, and he is hereby appointed a comittee to
take charge of and manage the estate of said
Elizabeth Wilson, according to law. He thereupon appeared in court and with J. T. Lawson

as his surety, who is accepted and approved
by the Court, executed bond as committee aforesaid, conditioned according to law. Eli
Marshall objects and excepts."

18/204 - October 12, 1889.
"Eli Marshall filed grounds and moved the court
for a new trial herein, and the court having
considered thereof orders that the motion be
overruled; to which the defendant, Eli Marshall,
excepts.
    Eli Marshall filed his Bill of Exceptions
herein, which was signed and sealed by the
Court and ordered to be made a part of the
record.
    Eli Marshall prayed an appeal to the Greenup
Circuit Court, which is granted him."

Wingo, Phoebe:
29/252 - March 19, 1874.
"It appearing to the satisfaction of the
court that Phoebe Wingo, a pauper lunatic,
was confined in the Greenup County Jail in
the custody and control of Charles Callihan,
Jailer for Greenup County, as her committee,
and had not sufficient estate for her support,
and no friends or parents to support her, and
that said pauper lunatic was taken care of
by said Jailer Callihan from the 31st day of
May 1873 to the 3rd day of June 1873, making
4 days.
    It is therefore ordered that the allowance
at the rate of $200.00 per annum be paid to
said Callihan for the proportionable time he
kept said pauper lunatic, which amounts to
the sum of $1.06 and that the same be certified
to the Auditor for payment under the Act
approved March 28, 1872."

Wood, John:
37/92 - April 6, 1893.
"An inquest upon John Wood, a lunatic, was
this day held and duly recorded."

39/383 - November 11, 1901.
"It appearing to the satisfaction of the
court that Mary Wheeler and John Wood, lunatics,
and Amos Carr, Cynthia Ann Burton, Minta

Traylor, John Traylor, Lucy Middaugh, Did
Nicholls, Isaiah Stepter, Minnie McGinnis,
and Mary Griffith, idiots, are still alive,
in the care of their committees, and have not
estate sufficient for their support, and that
their parents are still unable to support them."

Wurts, George:
35/118 - August 27, 1885 (age 14).
   "Upon motion of the attorney for the Commonwealth, it is ordered that a writ of de idiota
inquirendo issue in the case of George Wurts,
an idiot, returnable immediately, to inquire
into the state of mind of said George Wurts,
and it is ordered that D. J. McCoy, Esq., be
appointed counsel for said Wurts. Whereupon
came a jury, towit: C. H. Callon, W. S. Withrow, Jacob Rake, James Clifton, L. L. Mitchell,
R. D. Walker, Newton Crisp, David Floyd, John
H. Chinn, Thaddeus Bennett, and W. T. Hartley,
who being sworn according to law returned the
following verdict: 'We of the jury find from
the evidence that George Wurts is a person
of unsound mind and an idiot; that the unsoundness of mind has existed from birth; that he
was born in Greenup County and resides in
Greenup County, and is 14 years old; that he
was not brought into this state for the purpose
of becoming a charge upon the Commonwealth;
that he owns no estate of any kind; that his
father is living and mother is living and reside
in Greenup County, Kentucky, and they have
not estate sufficient to support the person
under trial, and said George Wurts is not capable of laboring in whole or in part for his
support.' (signed) W. S. Withrow, foreman.
   It is therefore ordered that Lewis Nicholls
be appointed a committee to take charge of
said George Wurts and provide him with suitable
diet, clothes, etc., and that he be allowed
therefor at the rate of $75.00 per annum, to
be paid upon further order of the court."

39/71 - November 9, 1899.
   "William Young tendered his resignation as
committee for George Wurts, an idiot, and it
is ordered that said resignation be accepted.
Ordered that Sam W. Peters be and he is hereby

appointed committee for said George Wurts.
He thereupon appeared in Court and took the
oath required by law, and together with H.
W. Peters, who is accepted and approved by
the court as his surety, executed bond to the
Commonwealth of Kentucky as committee aforesaid,
conditioned according to law."

39/390 - November 12, 1901.
    "It appearing to the satisfaction of the
court that George Wurts, an idiot, is still
alive, in the care of his committee, and has
not estate sufficient for his suport, and that
his parents are still unable to support him,
it is ordered that the allowance of $75.00
per annum for his support be continued from
the last payment, and that the same be copied
and certified to the Auditor of Public Accounts
for payment."

Wurts, William:
36/238 - February 25, 1890.
    "It appearing to the satisfaction of the
court that Mary Wheeler, Celia Leathers, John
Murphy, Malinda Carr, Did Nicholls, Grant
Damarin, William Wurts, and James A. Kitts,
idiots, are still alive, in the care of their
committee, and have not sufficient estate for
their support, and that their parents are still
unable to support them, it is ordered that
the allowance of $75.00 per annum be continued
from the last payment, and that the same be
copied and certified to the Auditor of Public
Accounts."

www.ingramcontent.com/pod-product-compliance
Lightning Source LLC
Chambersburg PA
CBHW070916270326
41927CB00011B/2595